THE YOUTH OF VIRGIL

LONDON : HUMPHREY MILFORD
OXFORD UNIVERSITY PRESS

PIETOLE VECCHIO IN 1800

THE YOUTH OF VIRGIL

BY

BRUNO NARDI

TRANSLATED BY BELLE PALMER RAND

WITH A PREFACE BY
EDWARD KENNÁRD RAND

CAMBRIDGE
HARVARD UNIVERSITY PRESS
1930

PRINTED IN THE U.S.A.

PREFACE TO THE TRANSLATION

PROFESSOR NARDI'S little book, "La Giovinezza di Virgilio" (Mantua, 1927), is here presented in an English version, with corrections and enlargements by the author. It deserves a wide circulation as one of the best brief accounts in existence of Virgil's youthful career and of the historical background both of the *Eclogues* and of whatever poetry had preceded that work. No two Virgilians will agree on all points in anybody's interpretation of the *Eclogues* or of the minor poems contained in the so-called *Appendix Vergiliana*, but any candid scholar will admire the skill with which Professor Nardi has sifted the bewildering array of information and misinformation in the ancient commentators, and the wise caution with which he has avoided the lure of plausible hypothesis. He would cheerfully admit that on various matters the last word remains to be spoken, if spoken it ever can be. Meanwhile his book will be found a useful addition to school and college libraries and will enlighten Virgilian scholars on not a few points. All may enlarge and some may even modify the opinions that they have rigorously entertained before. *Crede experto.*

A special point of interest, in view of recent discussions, is the appendix on Virgil's birthplace. This section of the book has been revised and enlarged by Professor Nardi expressly for the present translation. The reader will there find a most scholarly defence of the hoary tradition that identified the ancient Andes with Pietole. It may profitably be read in connection with the little volume *In Quest of Virgil's Birthplace* published by the undersigned with the Harvard University Press. The same Press issued in 1928 the notable work *Harvard Lectures on the Vergilian Age* by Professor Conway, who is sponsor for the novel view that the poet was born at Calvisano, or Carpenedolo. However the question is decided, the writers of all these books agree in their devotion to Virgil and in their eagerness to find the truth about him.

The translation was made with great care and fidelity by Mrs. Rand. This I have revised with slight changes in the language and in the style of footnote references. But in no case have I intentionally deviated from Professor Nardi's meaning; I have sought only to make it as intelligible as possible to English-speaking readers.

E. K. RAND

CONTENTS

APPENDICES

LIST OF WORKS FREQUENTLY CITED

Brummer: Iacobus Brummer, *Vitae Vergilianae*, Leipsic,
1912.

Carreri: Ferruccio Carreri, "Pietole, Formigada e il Fossato di Virgilio," in *Atti e Memorie della R. Accademia Virgiliana di Mantova* (1904), pp. 19–82. The
pages cited in the notes are those of the extract from
this work.

Cartault: Augustin Cartault, *Étude sur les Bucoliques
de Virgile*, Paris, 1897.

Diehl: Ernst Diehl, *Die Vitae Vergilianae und ihre antiken
Quellen*, Bonn, 1911.

Schanz: M. Schanz, *Geschichte der römischen Litteratur*
(Ivan von Müller's *Handbuch der klassischen Alter-
tumswissenschaft*, VIII), II, 1, §§ 218–250 (on Virgil
and his commentators). Page references are to the
third edition, 1911.

Thilo and Hagen: *Servii Grammatici qui feruntur in Vergilii Carmina Commentarii*, recensuerunt Georgius
Thilo et Hermannus Hagen, Leipsic, 1881–1902.
Vols. I–II contain Servius (with the enlarged form
"Servius Danielis," which may be Donatus) on the
Aeneid; III, 1 contains Servius on the *Bucolics and
Georgics;* III, 2 *Appendix Serviana* (by Hagen) contains the other ancient commentaries on Virgil except the *Scholia Bernensia.* These were published
by Hagen in *Fleckeisen's Jahrbuch*, Supplement-
band IV (1861–67), 675 ff. Their matter will also
be found in the commentary of Philargyrius with
the apparatus on the same in the *Appendix Serviana.*

The text of Virgil cited in the translation is that of
F. A. Hirtzel, *P. Vergili Maronius Opera*, in *Scriptorum
Classicorum Bibliotheca Oxoniensis*, Oxford, 1900. The
metrical renderings are from Theodore Chickering Wil-
liams, *The Georgics and Eclogues of Virgil, translated into
English verse*, Harvard University Press, 1915.

TO THE READER

THE little book which here sees the light, at the suggestion of the community of which the village of Pietole is a small part, does not pretend to make a new contribution to the already copious literature about Virgil. In writing it, my only intention has been, now that the second millennium of his birth approaches, to take my modest share in the honors that Mantua bestows upon that son of hers who brought her so much glory.

It seemed to me labor not entirely lost to collect the information scattered throughout the ancient biographies about the poet's early life, spent in greater part *inter flumina nota* upon his natal soil, until the storm broke that tore him from it. The reader will perceive that in the following pages special prominence has been given to the acounts that deal with Mantua. I must confess, moreover, that in presenting them, I have often found myself in sympathy with the Mantuan point of view. Civic pride? Let the gentle reader judge.

I have reduced citations to a minimum. Often, so as not to encumber the pages with notes, I have limited myself to a reference to the manual of Schanz, which is rich in bibliographies. I would

THE YOUTH OF VIRGIL

I. Mantua Me Genuit

Summary: 1. The glorification of Mantua. — 2. The parents of the Poet. — 3. The place, the time, and the legends about his birth. — 4. His education at Cremona, at Milan, and at Rome. His studies in rhetoric and philosophy. — 5. Virgil and the poets of the new school.

1

One does not read without emotion the verses which the Poet, at the beginning of the third book of the *Georgics*, dedicates to the Mantuan country. Turning to a subject not hitherto attempted by other poets, and feeling the bold security which comes to him through the matured virility of his art, he is no longer in need of training, but enters eagerly into the arena confident of the victory which will give immortal fame to him and to his distant country:

> temptanda via est, qua me quoque possim
> tollere humo victorque virum volitare per ora.
> Primus ego in patriam mecum, modo vita supersit,
> Aonio rediens deducam vertice Musas;
> primus Idumaeas referam tibi, Mantua, palmas,
> et viridi in campo templum de marmore ponam
> propter aquam, tardis ingens ubi flexibus errat
> Mincius et tenera praetexit harundine ripas.

In medio mihi Caesar erit templumque tenebit;
illi victor ego et Tyrio conspectus in ostro
centum quadriiugos agitabo ad flumina currus.[1]

Far from his sweet native land, although enjoy-
ing the comforts and favors with which his friends
and protectors overwhelmed him, he feels a nostal-
gic longing for Mantua, and with enamored fantasy
he sees again the verdant plain where the Mincio,
the river of his boyhood, winding in leisurely spi-
rals, broadens as it stretches out between its banks
all clothed in slender reeds. And now, if heaven
will permit him to live until his name shall fly from
mouth to mouth, the Poet makes solemn promise
to return some day to the obscure land of his fathers accompanied by the chorus of the Muses,
bearing as a gift the palm of victory which he shall
have gained by his song.

Was this, perhaps, the hope that Maecenas had
flashed before him, to encourage him in the arduous attempt? Later, when already sovereign poet,
he intoned the song of imperial Rome, and dared
to drag Homer in chains at the triumph of Augustus, not even then did he forget his fellow-citizens
beyond the Po. While still a youth, he had heard
at Cremona and at Milan tales of the deeds of Julius Caesar beyond the Alps; as a youth of twenty
at Rome he had heard the joyous acclamations ac-
corded to him in all the regions of Gaul where the

[1] *Georg.*, III, 8-15.

Roman toga had made its way;[1] he then had seen
the soldiers from beyond the Po follow the daring
leader in his march on Rome.[2] He thus could not
think that his compatriots were insensible to the
emprise of Aeneas, from which the Roman sover-
eignty originated and which had made the population beyond the Po equal to the conquerors of the
world. The Trojan hero, landing by the will of the
Fates on the shores of Latium, calls together the
Italian people favorable to him, and the Poet con-
ducts him into Etruria, among races that, kindred
to the Trojans, came from Lydia and were eager to
overthrow the tyrannical yoke of Mezentius, de-
spiser of the gods. Four troops of the Etruscans,
that is, the whole of Southern Etruria, seconded
the designs of Aeneas. And before long, Virgil adds
to them one troop of Ligurians and another of five
hundred Mantuans. This last troop is led by the
same Ocnus, son of the prophetess Manto and of
the Tuscan river Tiber. The legend, both popular
and sacred in character, concerning the Etruscan
origins of Mantua flourishes anew in the song of
the Poet and already, perhaps, gives signs of fusing
with the Theban legend as it will definitely do in
the accounts of the commentators. Ocnus had sur-

[1] Hirtius, *De bello gallico*, 51–52 (*omnes regiones Galliae
togatae*).
[2] Caesar, *De bello civili*, III, 87: "Hae copiae quas videtis, ex
delectibus horum annorum in citeriore Gallia sunt refectae, et
plerique sunt ex coloniis transpadanorum."

rounded the city with walls and had bestowed upon
it the name of his mother.

Rich in ancestors is Mantua, exclaims the Poet,
nor are all of the same stock. Three distinct races
live in its territory and each race is divided into
four peoples; Mantua controls all this population,
and the rule is in the hands of the Etruscan race.
After this rapid glance at the legends of his country, and at the conditions existing there before it
fell under the dominion of Rome, Virgil perceives
the ship laden with five hundred Mantuan warriors
set sail toward Latium through the waters of the
Mincio, born of its father Benacus, and from his
native river he sees once more the well-known
shores veiled with glaucous reeds.

> Ille etiam patriis agmen ciet Ocnus ab oris,
> fatidicae Mantus et Tusci filius amnis,
> qui muros matrisque dedit tibi, Mantua, nomen,
> Mantua dives avis, sed non genus omnibus unum:
> gens illi triplex, populi sub gente quaterni;
> ipsa caput populis, Tusco de sanguine vires.
> Hinc quoque quingentos in se Mezentius armat,
> quos patre Benaco velatus harundine glauca
> Mincius infesta ducebat in aequora pinu.[1]

It is the beautiful valley of the Po, dense with
woods, that comes spontaneously to the mind of
the Poet when his fantasy seeks vivid colors, fit
to portray the emerald greens of the blessed Ely-
sian Fields. A river divine is the Po, like the Nile,

[1] *Aen.*, X, 198–206.

the Euphrates, the Tigris, and the Ganges. It derives its waters, through a hidden channel, from a
fragrant wood of laurel in whose tranquil shades
the blest are joyfully feasting, or singing jocund
paeans. There are the heroes, who fighting for their
country suffer wounds, their heads bound with
snow-white fillets; there are the priests who lived
spotless lives and the bards who spoke words worthy of Phoebus and those who invented the glorious arts that cheer the life of man. The Eridanus
has its source among pleasant gardens bathed in
purple light in the eternal spring-time of the Ely-
sian Fields, and winds in and out among the woods
which shade its course and seem the earthly image
of the seats of the blessed.

> Conspicit ecce alios dextra laevaque per herbam
> vescentis laetumque choro paeana canentis
> inter odoratum lauri nemus, unde superne
> plurimus Eridani per silvam volvitur amnis.[1]

Never has poet, I think, felt more tender affection
for his native land, nor spoken words of finer praise.

2

In the fortunate land beyond the Po, in Andes,
a village three Roman miles distant from Mantua[2]
near the banks of the Mincio, was born Publius

---

[1] *Aen.*, VI, 656–659.
[2] See below, Appendix I.

Vergilius[1] Maro, on the Ides of October (the fifteenth), in the year 684 after the foundation of Rome (70 B.C.), in the first consulate of Gnaeus Pompey the Great and Marcus Licinius Crassus. His parents were country folk of modest condition according to the almost unanimous testimony of the ancient biographers, confirmed by a random remark in Macrobius.[2] However, this does not sig-

[1] About the original form of the name, whether *Virgilius* or *Vergilius*, our Humanists disputed learnedly; some supported the spelling common in the Middle Ages, while others, notably Politian, showed that *Vergilius* should be preferred. The dispute was protracted even to our times, and the bibliography of the discussion can be consulted, if one considers it worth while, in Fabricius, *Bibl. Lat.*, III, 152; in the chronological lives of De La Rue (*P. Virgilii Maronis historia de scripta per consules*, by Charles de la Rue (Ruaeus), in *P. Verg. Mar. Opera ad usum serenissimi Delphini* [Venetiis, 1713], vol. I.) and by Heyne (*P. Virg. Mar. vita per annos digesta*, in *P. Virg. Mar. Opera* [Turin: Pomba, 1827], vol. I). Stampini, *Georgiche di Virgilio commentate*, part 1 (Turin, 1884), pp. xvii ff.; Sabbadini in *Riv. di filol*, XXVII (1899), 93; and *Bolletino di filol.*, XIV (1907–08), 154; Schanz[3], II, 1, p. 35. The net result of the dispute is this: (1) that the most ancient manuscripts and inscriptions that are known from the second century before Christ to the fourth century of our era, have *Vergilius;* (2) that it was not until the fifth century that the form *Virgilius* came into use and the name was connected with *virga* or *virgo;* (3) that the popular form in Tuscan usage is *Vergilio* (one might also add that the dialectal form at Mantua is *Vergili*), while the literary and commonly accepted form is *Virgilio*. It is probable that among the Latins there was no uniform pronunciation, if Quintilian is correct in his observation about the promiscuous use of *e* and *i*, as in *Menerva* and *Minerva*, etc.

[2] *Saturnalia* V, 2, 1: "a Veneto rusticis parentibus nato inter silvas et frutices educto," etc. Only the *Vita Bernensis* puts Virgil higher in the social scale (Brummer, p. 66): "genere Mantuanus, dignitate eques Romanus."

nify that they were in desperate circumstances. As
for the occupation of the father, the elder Vergilius
Maro,[1] the ancients refer us to various sources
which, while not agreeing, are still not entirely con-
tradictory. Probus says simply that he was a peasant.[2] Donatus, however, informs us that according
to some he must have been a maker of terra cotta
vases, while according to other, and more numerous, authorities he was a hired man (not a slave, be
it said) of a certain Magius, a *viator*[3]— a carrier or
summoner, that is, for some local magistrate. The
same writer adds that by his ardor and diligence
Virgil's father so gained the esteem and affection
of his master, that he was given his daughter in
marriage. She, according to Probus and Focas was
called Magia Polla.[4] This marriage must have con-

[1] Virgil's father is referred to as Vergilius by Probus and
Servius, as Maro by Focas. The *Vita Monacensis* and the *Vita
Noricensis* call him Stimicon, following the allegorical interpretation of *Ecl.* V, in which Virgil is thought to have mourned the
death of his brother Flaccus. The verses in question are 54–55:
    "et puer ipse fuit cantari dignus et ista
    iam pridem Stimicon laudauit carmina nobis."

[2] Brummer, p. 73: "Patre Vergilio rustico."

[3] "P. Vergilius Maro Mantuanus parentibus modicis fuit ac
praecipue patre, quem quidam opificem figulum, plures Magi
cuiusdam viatoris initio mercennarium, mox ob industriam
generum tradiderunt egregiaeque substantiae silvis coemendis
et apibus curandis auxisse reculam." (Brummer, p. 1.) The
interpolated Donatus corrects the expression *egregiae substantiae* thus: "*quem cum agricolationi reique rusticae et gregibus
praefecisset,*" etc. (*Ibid.*, p. 20).

[4] Probus (Brummer, p. 73): "Natus . . . matre Magia Polla."
Focas (*Ibid.*, p. 50): "Mater Polla fuit, Magii non infima
proles."

siderably improved his condition; moreover, by leasing a bit of woods and cultivating bees, which at that time were rather plentiful in the Po valley, he increased his scanty substance bit by bit. Focas also calls him the cultivator of a small farm, possibly depending on no certain information but having in mind the poet's praises of country life in the *Georgics*.[1]

From the fact that the three names of the Poet are of Latin form, someone has inferred that his family had its origin in Central Italy.[2] There is no trace, however, of a definite statement of this sort in the ancient biographies, though Virgil is clearly called "Etruscan Bard" by the grammarian Focas,[3] and some, even, have discovered a certain Etruscan savor in the mother's name, Magia, and in that of the maternal grandfather, Magius.[4] Whatever there may be in this conjecture, it seems, nevertheless, that the Poet of the *Aeneid* took pleasure in attributing Etruscan origin to himself and to his city.

In this connection, then, it is profitable to inquire

---

[1] V, 30 (Brummer, p. 50): "hinc genitor figulus, Maro nomine, cultor agelli."

[2] Duchâtaux, *Virgile avant l'Enéide* (Paris, 1894), p. 15. See the *Vita Monacensis* (Brummer, p. 56): "Alii de Romanis, alii de Mantuanis parentibus natum autumant, infimis tamen."

[3] *Praef. ad vitam Verg.*, l. 22; *Vita*, l. 29 (Brummer, p. 50); *Vita Noricensis* (*Ibid.*, p. 55, l. 49).

[4] Cf. E. Diehl, *Die Vitae Vergilianae und ihre antiken Quellen* (Bonn, 1911), p. 9. From *Corp. Ins. Lat.*, vol. V it is evident that the name was rather frequent in the tenth Augustan region.

what was the ethnographical and political situation of Mantua, and in general of Transpadane Gaul, at the time of Virgil's birth. We have seen the Poet of the *Aeneid* boast of the Etruscan origin of his city, and of the supremacy the Etruscans maintained over the other two races, that of the Cenomanian Gauls, who probably had invaded the Mantuan territory up to the line of the Mincio, and that of the Veneti. Pliny also affirms that Mantua in his time was the only Etruscan city that remained beyond the Po.[1]

Now, it is known that the Cenomani and the Veneti were allies of the Romans from 225 B.C. on, in the war against the Gauls, who, after the first Punic War, had attempted a new invasion of Central Italy in the grand style. Some years later, Rome led her troops against the Insubri, and in 218 founded the first Latin colony in the Transpadane region at Cremona, where six thousand colonists of Central Italy were settled.[2] In 200 the Cenomani rebelled against the Romans, and together with the Insubri attempted a blow against Cremona. But, defeated in that year by the praetor L. Furius Purpureo and again in 197 by the consul C. Cornelius Cethegus on the banks of the

[1] *Nat. Hist.*, III, 23: "Mantua Tuscorum trans Padum sola reliqua."

[2] Polybius, *Hist.*, III, 40, 4-5. Cf. Pedroli, *Roma e la Gallia Cisalpina* (Turin, 1893), p. 102; Sigonio, *De antiquo iure Italiae*, II, c. 5.

Mincio, they turned friends of Rome and of her allies.

Meanwhile the Latin colony of Cremona in 190 B.C. was re-enforced by six thousand more families of colonists, who were to be dispersed throughout the surrounding territory. After the victory of Cethegus, Transpadane Gaul became thoroughly submissive to the Romans, who after 194 made with the various Celtic peoples pacts of friendship and alliance. A new Latin colony was founded in 183 B.C. at Aquileia for the purpose of preventing the Transalpine Gauls from invading the Venetian region, as they were trying to do. In the year 100, after the victory over the Cimbrians, a third Latin colony was established at Eporedia, the modern Ivrea.

This state of affairs in Transpadane Gaul, which in the meantime was invaded on all sides by colonists, merchants and tax-collectors from Rome, continued up to the end of 90 B.C., the year in which the Italic peoples, who for some time had been demanding equal rights with the Roman citizens, joined in a coalition and took up arms against Rome. The Social War, as it was called, proved the fidelity of the diverse communities to the Roman people. When the war was won by the Romans, the cities of Cisalpine Gaul which had not seceded or which, having revolted, had finally laid down their arms were gradually admitted to the benefits of Roman citizenship. Thus it came about that the Latin colony of Cremona was transformed into a *municipium*.[1]

In 89 B.C., as a result of the law proposed by Cn. Pompeius Strabo, father of Pompey the Great, there was granted to the municipal centres of Transpadane Gaul that had remained faithful to Rome the Latin rights (*ius Latii*), that is to say, the rights which the other Latin colonies possessed and which made eligible to the coveted citizenship those who had held some public office.[2] We do not know whether the law had effect or remained a simple promise made to prevent the defection of the Transpadane peoples. It is certain that agitations among these peoples did not cease, whether because they wished the promise kept, or because they demanded citizenship directly. Cicero informs us that C. Scribonius Curio, who was consul in 76 B.C., considered the demands of the Transpadane peoples as just, but affirmed that they should not be granted, for such an act would not be advantageous to the Republic.[3] Cicero does not say just when these re-

[1] Cf. Pedroli, *op. cit.*, I, 127.

[2] Asconius Pedianus, *In Pisonianam*, 3 (ed. A. C. Clark, Oxford, 1907), p. 3: "Pompeius enim non novis colonis eas [i.e. the Transpadane colonies] constituit, sed veteribus incolis manentibus ius dedit Latii, ut possent habere ius quod ceterae Latinae coloniae, id est, ut gerendo magistratus civitatem romanam adipiscerentur."

[3] *De Officiis*, III, 88: "Male etiam Curio, cum causam Transpadanorum aequam esse dicebat, semper autem addebat: 'Vincat utilitas!'"

quests were presented. We know, however, that in 66 the Transpadane peoples bestirred themselves to obtain Roman citizenship, and that Julius Caesar, resigning his office of quaestor before its expiration, repaired forthwith to the agitated communities.[1] Moreover, a year after, according to the explicit testimony of Cassius Dio, there arose a contest in Rome itself between two censors, one of whom, Marcus Crassus, held that citizenship should be conceded to the peoples beyond the Po, while his colleague opposed such action. Without reaching any conclusion, they resigned from office.[2]

How and when the Transpadanes were appeased we shall see a bit later. It may suffice for the present to have called attention to the above facts. The supposition that the parents of Virgil, especially his father, might have descended from the Latin colonists coming from Central Italy is certainly not absurd. Moreover, it might well agree with epigram VIII (X) of the *Catalepton*, which means, as some understand it, that the father of the Poet came from Cremona to establish himself in Mantua.[3] Still, this is a pure supposition.

[1] Suetonius, *Caes.*, 8.
[2] Cassius Dio, *Hist. Rom.*, XXXVII, 9.
[3]   "Villula quae Sironis eras et pauper agelle . . .
    commendo in primisque patrem, tu nunc eris illi
    Mantua quod fuerat, quodque Cremona prius."
(*Appendix Vergiliana* [ed. Ribbeck, 1868], p. 158). Cf. Duchâtaux, *op. cit.*, p. 17; Cartault, *Étude sur les Bucoliques de Virgile* (Paris, 1897), p. 4.

On the other hand, it seems difficult to imagine that Virgil, born and brought up as he was in a territory inhabited by a mixed and as yet unassimilated population, could be mistaken as to the ethnic character of his family. Virgil is called a Venetian in the passage of Macrobius already cited,[1] but for no other reason than that the writer has in mind the political and administrative division of Italy fixed by Augustus. In the same way Servius, a contemporary of Macrobius, and noted by the latter as the most learned grammarian of his time, makes Mantua a part of Venetia,[2] that is of the tenth Augustan region, to which Cremona and Brescia as Roman colonies were likewise assigned.[3]

3

As regards the place where Virgil first saw the light, most of his ancient biographers agree in mentioning Andes and in stating that this place was near the city.[4] They thus can call the Poet a Mantuan, and declare that he was born at Mantua, re-

[1] See above, p. 8, n. 2.

[2] "Civis Mantuanus (Vergilius), quae civitas est Venetiae" (Brummer, p. 68). "Origo Mantuanorum et a Tuscis venit, qui in Mantua regnabant, et a Venetis quia in Venetia posita est" (On *Aen.*, X, 201, Thilo and Hagen, II, 413). Cf. Sidonius, *Ep.*, IX, 15, l. 47: "Venetam lacessat ut favore Mantuam."

[3] Pliny, *Nat. Hist.*, III, 23, 130. Cf. Pedroli, *op. cit.*, pp. 96 ff.

[4] See Appendix I.

membering the well-known distich engraved on his
tomb. It has been ingeniously suggested that the
parents of Virgil were citizens of Mantua, but that
he was born by chance at Andes. But we cannot
accept this hypothesis, for the reason that according to the most ancient and most probable accounts the parents of the Poet were country people,
engaged in farming.[1] For the ancient biographers,
Virgil was Mantuan because Andes, where he was
born, was a place not far from the city. That he
also had in the city a house inherited from his maternal grandfather,[2] or acquired from his father,
who gradually had increased his scanty substance,
is certainly possible and agrees furthermore with a
Mantuan tradition.[3] But this, if it is true, does not
invalidate the testimony of the biographers and
the statement of Macrobius who calls Virgil "*a
rure Mantuano poetam.*"[4]

One difference has been noted among the ancient
biographers with regard to Andes; Donatus and St.
Jerome call Andes a *Pagus*, while Probus calls it a
Vicus.[5] A *pagus* is a country village that has land

---

[1] See above, pp. 8 f.

[2] Cartault, p. 6.

[3] Amadei, *Cronica di Mantova* (manuscript in the Reale
Archivo di Stato), I, 14; Portioli, *Monumenti a Virgilio in
Mantova* (Mantova, 1882), p. 14; Restori, *Mantova e dintorni.
Notizie storico-topografiche* (Mantova), p. 58.

[4] *Saturnalia*, V, 2, 1.

[5] Among the more recent biographers, the author of the
Vita Gudiana II (Brummer, p. 62) agrees with Donatus, while

about it called by its name, while a *vicus* is a cluster
of houses whether in a village or in a city. Ribbeck
and Cartault place more faith in Donatus, who has
as his source Suetonius.

The date of the Poet's birth is fixed by the well-
nigh complete agreement of his biographers, as the
Ides of October, the fifteenth of the month. Their
statement, further, is supported by other writers.[1]
It would seem that this date was taken from the
sepulchral inscription which was still legible at the
end of the first century after Christ. Moreover,
Heyne holds that Virgil's birthday was solemnized
by poets, as Martial[2] and Ausonius[3] attest. Certain
it is that Silius Italicus, accustomed not only to
preserve books, statues, and images of the ancient
authors, but also to venerate them, was particularly zealous in paying homage to Virgil. He was
wont to observe the Poet's birthday with greater
solemnity than his own, especially if he chanced to

the *Vita Noricensis* agrees with Probus, but refers also to St.
Jerome (*Ibid.*, pp. 54–55). The *Vita Monacensis* (*Ibid.*, p. 56)
has "*in pago Andensi in villa quae Andis dicitur iuxta Mantuam*" (*Ibid.*, p. 56); the *Vita Gudiana* III (*Ibid.*, p. 64): "*in
oppido prope Mantuam.*"

[1] Diehl, p. 9; Cartault, p. 2; Heyne, p. lxii; Ribbeck, *De vita
et scriptis P. Vergili Maronis*, in *P. Vergili Maronis Opera
in usum scholarum* (Leipsic: Teubner, 1884), p. viii.

[2] *Epigr.*, XII, 67:
　　　　"Octobres Maro consecravit Idus.
　　　　Idus saepe colas et has et illas
　　　　qui magni celebras Maronis Idus."

[3] *Idyll.*, V, 25 (ed. Peiper, p. 259):
　　　　"Octobres olim genitus Maro dicat Idus."

18   THE YOUTH OF VIRGIL

be at Naples, where he was accustomed to visit the
tomb of the Poet as if it were a temple.[1]

The birth of such a man as Virgil could not be re-
counted like that of an ordinary mortal, and Donatus has transmitted to us the legends which flourished at an early date around his cradle and were
amplified by popular fancy and the fancy of the
commentators. The first concerns the prophetic
dream of the Poet's mother. Donatus relates that
when she was with child, she dreamed of giving birth
to a branch of laurel, which, on touching the soil,
took root and grew quickly into a mature tree laden
with various fruits and flowers.[2] This is one of the
usual themes which from the dream of Hecuba to
that of the mother of St. Dominic is found in numerous stories of heroes and saints, and has even
created copious pseudo-philosophical literature.
The presence of this legend in the ancient biographies of Virgil is a proof of the esteem in which the
Poet was held from the first century of our era.

The second legend in Donatus is a sequel to the
first. The day after the dream, Virgil's mother,

[1] Pliny, *Epist.*, III, 7.

[2] See Brummer, p. 1 and (for Philargyrius), p. 40. Focas
puts part of the story into verse (ll. 37–43, Brummer, p. 50).
In the *Vita Noricensis* and the *Vita Monacensis* the laurel bough
grows into a terebinth and Magia has the dream interpreted
to her by her brother — none less than the poet Lucretius
(*Ibid.*, pp. 54, 56)! *Vita Gudiana* I presents a garbled combina-
tion of these two versions (*Ibid.*, p. 60). Philargyrius (Thilo
and Hagen, III, 2, p. 59) speaks of Magia's dream in the comment on *Ecl.* III, 62.

while walking in the country with her husband, was
stricken with the pangs of child-birth. She left the
road and was delivered in a ditch.[1] This story contains nothing extraordinary in itself, but shows its
legendary origin by being so closely connected with
the fable of the dream which precedes it and with
the fantastic details that follow it. Pascoli thinks
that the ditch of the legend was a furrow for grain,
and argues this from the fact that Virgil was born
at seed-time, the fifteenth of October. It does not
appear, however, that Focas understands it thus,
for he relates that the verdant earth furnished flowers for the little boy and with a spring-time gift
made ready for him a grassy couch.[2] The idea of
the ditch is meant rather to suggest the mother's
modesty than the season of the year. Pascoli's interpretation presupposes that some commentator
had taken his inspiration for the legend from a
theme in the *Georgics*, as though the birth of Virgil
in a furrow of the grain-field were a happy augury
for him who was to sing the marvellous song:

> What brings glad harvest-days, what starry sign
> Bids turn the sod for seeding, when to wed
> The elm tree and the vine.

---

[1] Brummer, p. 2: "in subiecta fossa partu levata est." The
London manuscript and that of Brussels (*Ibid.*) have: "in
foveam divertit ibique peperit."

[2] Lines 50 f. (Brummer, p. 51):
> "terra ministravit flores et munere verno
> herbida supposuit puero fulmenta virescens."

This hypothesis seems to me scarcely probable; I prefer the more natural one of Sonntag, who derives this legend from that told by Donatus about the poplar, of which I shall speak presently and which very probably contains an element of truth.

Meanwhile Donatus has a third legend to narrate. The moment that Virgil saw the light, he uttered no infant cry, but his face bore so mild a look as to give no uncertain hope of his high destiny.[1] It seemed to the commentators that the predestined boy, from whose lips was to pour forth such serene poetry, could not like other baby boys emit strident cries and wrinkle his little face in grotesque grimaces. Oh, "scholars and men of letters," whom Dante condemned to walk in the burning sand under a rain of fire as expiation for having defied the holy laws of nature!

The fourth legend related by Donatus as a prophecy, is that of the poplar. In the very spot where Virgil was born, there was planted, after the custom of the country, a poplar switch, which grew so quickly that it attained the height of poplars planted long before. This poplar, relates Donatus, was called Virgil's tree, and was venerated with

---

[1] Brummer, p. 2. Focas adds to the preceding legends that of the bees who settled in the mouth of the little boy and made there a honeycomb (*Ibid.*, p. 51, ll. 47-48, 52-56). The legend of the bees, taken from the life of Plato, is truly precious, for it gives us tangible evidence of the manner in which certain imaginary details, partly pleasing and partly absurd, have clustered about the story of the Poet's life.

utter devotion by women with child, who offered prayers before it.[1] In this legend there is perhaps a nucleus of truth, namely, the use of the spot and the existence of a tree of Virgil venerated in the natal place of the Poet in the time of Suetonius, upon whom Donatus depends. It is also probable that this amount of historical fact gave rise not only to this legend but likewise to the other, which represents the Poet as born in the fields, in a ditch near the poplar that was sacred to his memory. This poplar planted in his honor, on his natal soil, according to the custom of the country, might induce one to believe that it stood there to mark the spot where Virgil was born. Possibly, thinks Sonntag,[2] his detractors whispered the story about in order to give color to the rumor that the Poet was the son of vagabonds.

But besides reviewing these bits of legend, it is worth while to stop for an instant to consider the historical moment at which the Poet was born, who, in his youth, felt himself impelled to sing of the mar-

[1] Brummer, p. 2: "Accessit aliud praesagium, si quidem virga populea more regionis in puerperiis eodem statim loco depacta ita brevi evaluit, ut multo ante satas populos adaequavisset, quae arbor Vergilii ex eo dicta atque etiam consecrata est summa gravidarum ac fetarum religione et suscipientium ibi et solventium vota." Cf. Focas, ll. 59–64 (*Ibid.*, p. 51) and the *Vita Gudiana* I (*Ibid.*, p. 60). The *Vita Noricensis*, instead of a *virga populea* has a *palmes* (*Ibid.*, p. 55).

[2] *Vergil als bukolischer Dichter* (Leipsic, 1891), pp. 239, 240. Sonntag's argument is plausible enough without his suggestion of the part played by Virgil's detractors.

vellous feats of the Roman people, and in his matu-
rity made Rome the rival of Greece in epic poetry.
In the year before the birth of Virgil, Pompey the
Great won the long and dangerous war in Spain
against Sertorius, and laden with glory returned to
Rome, together with Licinius Crassus the Rich,
whom he had aided in subduing the last strong-
holds in which the rebellious slaves of Spartacus
were sheltered from the storm. The two illustrious
captains, forming an agreement to keep the government of the republic in their hands, demanded the
consulate, and in the following year obtained it.
There was urgent need of bridling the autocratic
régime, which the senatorial oligarchy, heir of the
dictatorship of Sulla, imposed on all classes of so-
ciety. Once consuls, Pompey and Crassus ener-
getically set about the work of reform. The Sullan
constitution was abolished, the Senate purified, the
equites and the people had their rights restored.
Only under the consulate of these two strong men
of state was it possible to revive the censorship, an
office which had become odious to the Romans and
had in fact been abolished for some fifteen years.
The censors of that year, L. Gellius and Cn. Lentu-
lus, had taken the census of the Roman citizens,
which was found to amount to 450,000. They then
arranged for the celebration of the 67th lustrum, a
rite which was wont to be proclaimed every five
years in the Campus Martius, after the census; its

purpose was at once financial — to collect tributes
—and religious — to purify the people by the sac-
rifice of a triple victim, pig, sheep, bull (*suovetauri-
lia*). It was just in this year and at this moment of
the history of Rome, that there was born in an obscure village of Transpadane Gaul the great master
of Latin poetry, who in his songs was destined to
transmit to us a lasting echo of the Roman events
of his times.

4

Of the education which Virgil received in his
early youth we have very scant information. Donatus tells us that the Poet passed at Cremona the
first years of his life, up to his assumption of the
toga virilis.[1] Literally taken, the words of the grammarian would lead us to suppose that Virgil's family
was of Cremona, in disagreement with what the
same author has stated a little earlier. To avoid
this contradiction, one must admit either that Donatus has badly summarized Suetonius or that the
words *initia aetatis* are taken in a very broad sense.[2]

[1] "Initia aetatis Cremonae egit usque ad virilem togam quam
septimo decimo anno natali suo accepit isdem illis consulibus
iterum [duobus], quibus erat natus, evenitque ut eo ipso die
Lucretius poeta decederet" (Brummer, p. 2). The words *septimo decimo* have been restored by me on the testimony of the
manuscripts in place of the number XV adopted by Reifferscheid.

[2] Cartault, pp. 9 f.

From the phase used by Evangelus in Macrobius,
though something may be discounted from the
acerbity of this disparager of the Poet, Virgil would
seem to have grown up in the woods and bushes
that surrounded his native village.[1] All this agrees
very well with the laconic notice which St. Jerome
takes straight from Suetonius and records under
the year 58 B.C.: *Vergilius Cremonae studiis eruditur.*[2]

At the age of twelve, then, Virgil was taken to
Cremona, it would seem, to receive there a training
in letters; this would certainly not have happened
if his father had not had the means, or if someone
else, recognizing the talent of the boy, had not
taken charge of his studies. Perhaps it was at this
time that his family followed him to Cremona;[3] the
city, which had been for some thirty years a Roman
municipium and a centre for the Romanization of
Transpadane Gaul, must have had schools to teach
boys at least the first rudiments of grammar. There
he would have had opportunity to study those subjects which according to Quintilian[4] were taught in
the first grade and were designated by the name of
grammar. At Cremona, Virgil assumed the *toga*

---

[1] *Saturnalia,* V, 2, 1: "inter silvas et frutices educto."

[2] *Chron., Olymp.* CLXXX, 3 (ed. Schoene, II, 137).

[3] That is, if I correctly understand the verse already cited
from *Catal.,* VIII (X) (unless the poem is an anonymous exer-
cise): "tu nunc eris illi | Mantua quod fuerat quodque Cremona
prius," where *prius* may refer to Mantua and Cremona together,
as opposed to *nunc.*

[4] *Inst. Or.,* I, 4-9.

virilis. But on this point, there is evidently a contradiction in the manuscripts of the *Life* by Donatus. For although they all agree in stating that Virgil was seventeen years old (and that was his age in
53 B.C.), they then add, with two sole exceptions,
that the event took place in the second consulate
of Pompey and of Crassus, in 55. Reifferscheid,
who does not agree with the clear statement repeated from Suetonius by Donatus, believed it easy,
with a little leniency, to eliminate the discrepancy
correcting the "seventeen" in the manuscripts into
XV. But the trouble is that St. Jerome, who is also
said to depend on Suetonius, informs us that in 53
Virgil, having assumed the *toga virilis*, went to
Milan.[1]

In the laconic style of the *Chronicon* of Eusebius,
completed by St. Jerome, it would seem that the
departure for Milan took place at the same time as
the assumption of the *toga candida.* Further to en-
tangle the skein, and to render still more evident
the contradiction in the manuscripts of Donatus,
the latter also state that on the same day that
Virgil assumed the *toga virilis*, the poet Lucretius
died. It would be easy to say that we are concerned
with the invention of a grammarian, who endeav-
ors by means of this coincidence to make Virgil the
successor of Lucretius in dactylic poetry.[2] How-

[1] Cf. below, p. 26.
[2] Cartault, p. 10.

ever, this statement is derived from the same source
from which St. Jerome draws his information. He,
in fact, without indicating the precise year, records
under Olympiad 171 the birth of Lucretius, who,
he adds, died by his own hand at the age of 44 (or
according to some manuscripts, 43).[1] Let us place
the birth of Lucretius in the first year of the 171st
Olympiad, that is in 97 B.C.; if he died at the age
of 44, the act occurred precisely 53 B.C., when
Virgil, who was seventeen years of age, left Cremona for Milan.[2]

To those ancients who noted this coincidence, it
very probably had a deep meaning; but the coincidence itself presupposes in those who have noted it
a calculation based on historical data which at that
time were not lacking. The text of Donatus as it
has come down to us betrays evident retouches
from someone who has attempted to combine two
accounts, probably from different sources, without
knowing the exact chronology of the events. For
this reason, I believe it would be preferable to leave
Donatus' statement exactly as it is.[3]

[1] Hier., *Chron.*, *Olymp.* CLXXI, 3 (ed. Schoene, II, 133).

[2] But another calculation is also possible. Let us place the
birth of Lucretius in the first year of the 171st Olympiad. If
he died in his 43d year (*quadragesimo tertio aetatis suae anno*,
according to some manuscripts of St. Jerome), or in his 42d,
this might well have happened in 55 B.C., when Pompey and
Crassus were consuls for the second time.

[3] Meanwhile two things give me food for thought. First
there is the testimony of the two manuscripts C and K whose
text is reproduced by Brummer. He calls them twins, although

Whether he assumed the *toga virilis* at fifteen or seventeen, Virgil finished his first studies at Cremona and was then sent away to Milan. But he remained in this city only a short time, and after a brief stay there, proceeded to Rome.[1]

To attest the flourishing condition of education at Milan, a letter of Pliny the Younger is generally cited which, written more than a century after Virgil went there, informs us that the youth of Como went to Milan to study because in their city there were no schools.[2] Perhaps, however, Virgil did not find there better teachers than he had left at Cremona —hence his short stay there. But he must have also been impelled toward Rome by the ardent desire to know near at hand the city which exercised even from afar so great a fascination on his spirit. We have referred to the agitations among

C is of the twelfth and K of the thirteenth century, and considers them extracts from the *Life* by Donatus. At all events, they make every contradiction disappear by omitting any reference to the second consulate of Pompey and to the coincidence with the death of Lucretius; they affirm simply that Virgil assumed the toga at the age of seventeen. And then the absolute silence of Focas surprises me somewhat, since he speaks neither of the studies of Virgil at Cremona and at Mantua, nor of the *toga virilis;* he seems to make the lad's first teacher one Ballista, of whom we shall speak later, and who from the context would seem to be a Mantuan.

[1] Donatus (Brummer, p. 2): "Sed Vergilius a Cremona Mediolanum et inde paulo post transiit in urbem." "Vergilius sumpta toga Mediolanum transgreditur et post breve tempus Romam pergit." Hier., *Chron., Olymp.* CLXXXI, 4 (ed. Schoene, II, 133).

[2] *Epist.,* IV, 13.

the population beyond the Po to obtain Roman
citizenship. The Celts and the Etruscans who inhabited Transpadane Gaul, now turned their eyes
and hearts toward Rome, which in the fiery crucible
of her power was melting the diverse races of the
peninsula to make of it one country. The very year
that Virgil, at the age of twelve, went to Cremona,
Julius Caesar assumed for five years powers extraordinary over the Gallic provinces, which powers
the Vatinian law had conferred upon him, together
with four legions; and at the expiration of this time,
his command was confirmed again for another period of five years. When he had undertaken the
conquest of Transalpine Gaul, Caesar made Cisalpine Gaul the base for his re-equipment of militia.
And since the peoples of Northern Italy were faithful to him, he was very liberal to them in concessions and in promises. He founded a colony of
5000 householders at Cremona and conferred citizenship upon this city.[1] In 52 the insistent report
circulated that he had likewise, on his own initia-
tive, granted to the other cities beyond the Po the
rights of suffrage and tenure of office.[2] This act

[1] Strabo, V, 1, 6; Cicero, *Ad Fam.*, XIII, 35; Pedroli,
p. 136.

[2] Cicero, *Ad Att.*, V, 2, 3 (April 10, 52; May 10, 51 according
to Purser): "eratque rumor de Transpadanis eos iussos (i.e.
by Caesar) III viros creare." He also refers, in the following
May (*Ad Fam.*, VIII, 1, 2, about May 22, 51, according to
Purser) to the "*rumores de comitiis Transpadanorum.*" Cf.
Pedroli, p. 135.

served as a pretext for the attack launched against
him at Rome by the aristocratic party, which had
resolved to take away from him the command of
the Gallic provinces.

While these things were happening in his native
country, perhaps in 52 B.C., Virgil, at the age of
eighteen, was making his entrance into the city of
which he had heard so much, into the city which to
his poetic fancy seemed to lift her proud brow above
all other cities, Mantua in particular, even as the
cypresses above the pliant viburna.[1]

When he arrived at Rome, events decisive for the
history of the world were maturing in the city. The
struggle between the party of the nobility and that
of the people had entered into the most acute phase.
Armed bands under the command of Clodius for
the plebeian party and of Milo for the aristocratic
party, two demagogues of the same stamp, ran with
impunity about the streets of the city and its sub-
urbs, spreading terror with riot and rapine and
unprecedented assassinations. All security of person and of property had failed; intrigues and de-
ceptions and threats had become habitual. The
annual committee for the election to the consulate
and other offices of the republic had been rendered
impossible. Pompey the Great, the only triumvir
present at Rome, could have put a restraint on the
dominant demagogy and general disorder, and he

[1] *Ecl.* I, 19-25.

seemed to take pleasure in the condition of affairs
with the hope of being invoked as savior. Already,
in the course of the year 53 B.C., a tribune of the
people had proposed to confer the dictatorship upon
him, but the plan failed on account of the opposition of Cato. Of the other two triumviri, the one,
Licinius Crassus, had been killed in the war against
the Parthians; the other, Caesar, was engaged in
putting down the revolt of Vercingetorix. In Rome,
at the beginning of 52, the consular elections were
postponed and an interregnum was created. Then
it was that, on the road which led from Rome to
Lanuvium, the band of Milo, who aspired to the
consulate, met with that of Clodius, who was openly
intriguing against him. The encounter took place
at Bovillae and Clodius was slain. His body was
carried to Rome by his partisans. They erected for
him at the forum a funeral pyre of the furniture
and seats of the Senate-house.

To calm the tumult which followed, the Senate,
toward the end of February, conferred the consulate on Pompey, who entered immediately into
office without a colleague. Thus the great general
put himself openly at the head of the Senatorial
party averse to Caesar, and in the meantime began
to enroll militia in Italy on his own account. The
popular party favorable to Caesar saw clearly into
the plans of Pompey, who, accused of aspiring to
the dictatorship, was constrained in the last five

months of his consulship to associate himself with
a colleague in the person of his father-in-law, Q.
Metellus Scipio. For the purpose of frustrating the
underhand dealings of his colleague, now openly become his adversary, Caesar presented through the
tribunes his *petitio absentis* for a second consulship.
This petition consisted in requesting that at the
expiration of the ten years which ought by law to
intervene between the first and second consulship,
he should be permitted to present his own candidacy, without surrendering his command of Gaul or
coming personally to Rome as was the custom. At
first, nobody perceived that the request of Caesar
involved an extension of his Gallic command, desired by him to obviate the action plotted against
him; it therefore received the support of Pompey
and Cicero. When, however, Pompey saw the snare
in which his adversary had involved him, he en-
deavored to annul the concession. The following
year, the consul M. Claudius Marcellus proposed
to the Senate without more ado that Caesar should
be recalled from the Gauls to prevent his making
use of the privilege obtained, and at the same time
he insisted that the rights of Roman citizenship
which Caesar had conceded to the colonists of
Como should be taken from them. Caesar sought
to put to the vote the proposals of Marcellus, bar-
tered the influence which he had with his colleague,
Sulpicius Rufus, and above all secured the opposi-

tion of the tribune elect, C. Scribonius Curio, whom
he had won over by bribery to his cause. The question dragged on into the following year, under the
consulate of Aemilius Lepidus and C. Claudius
Marcellus. When a definite plan was demanded,
Curio proposed that the command of the Gauls
should be taken from Caesar but at the same time
Pompey should be relieved of his command in
Spain. Then, as soon as the proposal was voted on
and approved for Caesar but not for Pompey, the
tribune put a veto on the law and thus was Caesar
saved.

Caesar, meanwhile, after he had secured by
means of generous concessions the obedience of the
population recently subdued by him, hastened at
the end of winter into Cisalpine Gaul, where he was
received with great pomp and ceremony by all the
municipalities and colonies. The roads, the public
squares, the houses, wherever Caesar passed, were
decorated as for a holiday; the people in crowds
rushed toward him acclaiming him; sacrifices were
offered in his honor, and there was feasting in the
fora and in the temples. It was on this population,
exultant and proud to obey him, that the conqueror of the Gauls relied to win the match in
which he and Pompey were about to engage.

With the pretext that the Parthians were threat-
ening the Roman province of Syria the Senate had
ordered Pompey and Caesar to surrender each a

legion to be sent to the East. On this occasion
Pompey demanded of Caesar the legion which he
had given over to him two years before. Thus
Caesar saw himself suddenly deprived of two legions, which instead of being sent against the Parthians were retained by Pompey in Italy. Moreover, Caesar's candidate for the consulship for the
year 49 B.C., S. Galba, had been beaten in the elections, an event of which the aristocrats made great
boast. Caesar, who in the meantime had placed his
camp at Ravenna, saw that the moment for the ir-
revocable decision had arrived. Toward the end of
50 B. C. he sent to Rome a letter, his ultimatum,
which was to be read in the Senate the first of January, 49. The conciliating proposals offered by him
were not accepted, and on the seventh of January,
full powers for the defence of the Republic were
conferred on the consuls, and Caesar was declared
an enemy of the state. It was open strife, civil war,
which was to depopulate Rome, put an end to the
aristocratic régime, and make of Caesar the per-
petual dictator, the chief. On the eleventh of January, he cast the fatal die. Crossing the Rubicon, he
marched on Rome, from which, on the eighteenth
of the same month, the consuls and the magistrates
fled in the tracks of Pompey, who was destined no
more to set foot therein.

It was in the midst of the events of the first three
months of 705 A.U.C. (49 B.C.), that, in accord-

ance with the explicit testimony of Cassius Dio,[1]
Caesar conceded to the Gauls between the Po and
the Alps the long-desired gift of Roman citizenship.
The new municipalities created in the region were
assigned to some one of the tribes into which the
Roman citizens had been divided; thus, while Ve-
rona was assigned to Poblilia, and Brescia and
Padua to Fabia, which was the tribe of Caesar,
Mantua, on the other hand, was admitted to the
tribe of Sabatina.[2]

Just what Virgil did when he arrived in Rome,
and how long he remained there, we do not know.
Probus, without speaking of the youth's journey
to Rome, affirms merely that he pursued his studies
of rhetoric under the guidance of the greatest masters.[3] The *Vita Bernensis* gives the name of one of
thesemasters,the rhetor Epidius; it adds thatVirgil
had in school with him as a fellow-pupil, the young
Octavius, grand-nephew of Caesar and destined
heir to his political power.[4] This statement is perhaps made up from Suetonius, who informs us that

[1] *Hist.*, XLI, 36. Cf. Tacitus, *Ann.*, XI, 24. The *Lex Roscia*,
concerning the citizenship to be conferred on all Cisalpine Gaul,
is of the 11th of March, 49. This is followed, we do not know
exactly in what year, by the *Lex Rubria*, which gave to the new
citizens a precise organization and a rough model of a judicial
statute. (Pedroli, pp. 138f.)

[2] Kubitscheck, *De romanarum tribuum origine ac propagatione*
(Vienna, 1882), p. 88; Pedroli, p. 137.

[3] Brummer, p. 73, l. 4.

[4] Brummer, p. 67, ll. 6-7: "Ut primum se contulit Romae,
studuit apud Epidium oratorem cum Caesare Augusto."

Epidius, who was noted for his scurrilous discourses, founded a school and had as pupils Mark Antony and Augustus. This may well be true. Donatus also declares that Virgil had pursued the study of rhetoric and that he even pleaded a case in court,— once only, however; for he lacked, according to Melissus, the readiness of speech and the smooth eloquence of the lawyers.[1]

For that matter, the times were not propitious for declamation. Arms dominated the toga, and that very prince of Latin eloquence, Cicero, was preparing to bid farewell to the forum, to dedicate himself to philosophy, in which he sought consolation for his griefs. That to which the great orator was reluctantly impelled by grim necessity, the young Mantuan accepted with good grace; the divine harmonies that echoed in his soul became all the sweeter, the less he heard of rhetoricians' prattle. He gladly turned to the tranquil ports of human wisdom, under the teaching of the gentle Epicurus, whose interpreter in Rome was the great Siro.[2]

[1] Brummer, p. 4: "Egit et causam apud iudices, unam omnino nec amplius quam semel; nam et in sermone tardissimum ac paene indocto similem fuisse Melissus tradidit."

[2] *Catal.*, V (VII):

> "Ite hinc, inanes, ite, rhetorum ampullae . . .
> Ite hinc, inane cymbalon inventutis . . .
> nos ad beatos vela mittimus portus,
> magni petentes docta dicta Sironis,
> vitamque ab omni vindicabimus cura."

The authenticity of this composition, considered probable by Ribbeck and others, is doubted by Cartault, p. 15.

The name of Siro as Virgil's teacher in philosophy is given by Focas,[1] by Servius,[2] by Philargyrius,[3] and by Donatus.[4] Cicero also informs us that
in about the year 50, Siro was successfully teaching
the Epicurean philosophy in Rome, and he presents him and Philodemus to us as "most excellent
and learned men."[5] To some it appears that the
statements of the grammarians and scholiasts are
suspicious, since they are involved in a question-
able interpretation of the *Sixth Eclogue* and cited
to explain the friendship of Virgil with Alfenus
Varus. Without entering into the question, I will
note only that the appearance of the name of Siro
in those two poems of the *Catalepton*[6] shows that
even if they are not Virgil's the statement goes
back to a time very near to that of the Poet, and
was scarcely made up of whole cloth.[7] If, however,
the reconstruction proposed by Körte[8]of a passage
in the Herculaneum rolls is exact, Virgil in company
with Varius, Horace and Quintilius would seem to
be a pupil of that other Epicurean, Philodemus,
whom Cicero mentions with Siro.

[1] Brummer, p. 52, l. 87.
[2] On *Buc.*, VI, 13; *Aen.*, VI, 264.
[3] On *Buc.*, VI, 13.
[4] According to the Bodleian MS. (Brummer, pp. 32-33) and
the Vulgate text.
[5] *De Fin.*, II, 119; cf. *Ad Fam.*, VI, 11.
[6] V (VII) and VIII (X).
[7] On this question see Pascal, *Commentationes Vergilianae*
(Milan, 1900), pp. 43 ff.
[8] *Rhein. Mus.*, XLV (1890), 172-177.

That Virgil, after his experience in the schools of
rhetoric, had frequented one or more schools of
philosophy amongst the many opened in Rome by
learned Greeks, and particularly that Epicurean
school of Siro and of Philodemus, is not only possible but very probable. In this sense we may accept
the testimony of Probus that Virgil follows the
sect of Epicurus.[1] But that he was an Epicurean,
in the historical sense of the word, is a supposition
of the grammarians, who even so are not in complete agreement with one another. This supposition is founded principally on the interpretation of
the song of Silenus in the *Sixth Eclogue* and of certain passages in the *Georgics*, where the Epicureanism consists merely of reminiscences of Lucretius.[2]
The unknown interpolator of the Donatus *Life* in
the Bodleian manuscript understood better perhaps than the ancients, and some modern scholars,
Virgil's attitude toward philosophy, for he observes
that the Poet accepts in his works the doctrines of
different philosophers but that he shows his at-
tachment above all to Plato.[3]

[1] Brummer, p. 73, l. 10: "Secutus Epicuri sectam."

[2] As has been abundantly proved by Ronzoli, *La religione e
la filosofia di Vergilio* (Turin, 1900), pp. 64 ff.

[3] Brummer, p. 33: "Et quamvis diversorum philosophorum
opiniones libris suis inseruisse de animo maxime videatur, ipse
fuit Academicus; nam Platonis sententias omnibus aliis prae-
tulit." The electicism dominant in the philosophical culture of
that time, in Rome, is shown by the works of Cicero and of
Varro, not to mention the school of the Sestii, founded, perhaps, when Virgil was writing the *Bucolics*.

Donatus asserts that among his other studies
Virgil included that of medicine and especially that
of mathematics. These two subjects were not, as
in modern times, entirely distinct from philosophy;
rather they were generally considered parts of it.
If by mathematics celestial mathematics, that is,
astronomy, is meant, the testimony of Donatus
amounts precisely to this, that Virgil applied himself to the study of the philosophy of nature, indubitable traces of which are found in his writings.[1]
Without accepting the exaggerated conception that
the ancients had of his wisdom,[2] we can see that
his poetry has fed on solid learning, such as is found
in no other Latin poet, except Lucretius, to whom,
after Homer, Virgil owes so much.

5

But Virgil is, above all, a poet. It is not so important for us to be acquainted with his training in
letters and philosophy, as to know the environ-
ment in which his poetical temperament was gradually formed. At the moment when he arrived at
Rome, an energetic school of young poets was engaged in reforming both the spirit and the modes

[1] The following places are generally cited: *Buc.*, III, 40 ff.;
Georg., I, 32 ff., 204 ff., 231 ff.; II, 475 ff.; III, 478 ff.
[2] "Vergilius nullius disciplinae expers" (Macrobius, *In
Somn. Scip.*, I, 6, 44); "Savio gentil che tutto seppe" (Dante,
Inf., VII, 3).

of Latin poetry. Students and often imitators of
the Alexandrian models, full of the spirit of Hellen-
istic culture, which now had the upper hand, in
Roman education, over the stern traditions of the
good old times, they courted, as did later our Humanists, a type of pure and ideal beauty, free from
every moral and utilitarian bond, and created art
for art's sake. Cicero, tenaciously attached to Ennius, and in this respect an heir to the conservative
spirit of the elder Cato, cherished no sympathy for
the "new poets," whom, for their imitation of the
Alexandrines he called caustically "Singers of Euphorion." Nevertheless, the new manner was not
so much the result of imitation, as rather the expression of that profound revolution in ideas and
customs, which is the more intimate aspect of social
and political revolutions and explains them. The
greater refinement in the tenor of life, that which
historians call the "corruption" of the severe customs of the past, tended to induce and did induce
Roman artists, particularly the poets, to seek an
art more refined, richer in modes of expression and
of studied elegance. In fine, the imitation was
nothing other than a means for satisfying a need.
Nor did the Alexandrine manner dry up, in true
poets, their vein of originality; it welled forth in
the songs of Catullus and in the *Bucolics* of our
Mantuan.

Catullus, the poet of Verona, who had given so

much grace and lightness to the Latin lyric, was the
best representative of the new school of poetry.
But he died while still a youth, shortly after the
arrival of Virgil in Rome. There were still living,
however, friends of Catullus, young Bohemians who
poetized in the Alexandrian manner, and whose
names had acquired vogue among men of letters.
They were Licinius Calvus, Cornificius Gallus,[1]
Helvius Cinna,[2] the Transpadane, Furius Bibaculus and Quintilius Varus, both of Cremona, Valerius Cato, also from Northern Italy,[3] and probably
Asinius Pollio,[4] the future friend and protector of
Virgil. Among these was also a Greek poet, Parthenius, a native of Bithynia, who was particularly
attached to Cinna. The elegies of Parthenius were
imitated by Cornelius Gallus, coeval and fellow-
pupil with Virgil. Virgil himself, apparently, had
borrowed some of his verses — hence some have
inferred that the Mantuan Poet had had Parthenius as master.[5] In reality we do not know with
which one of these writers Virgil was intimate, during his first sojourn at Rome. What is certain is

[1] According to the *Scholia Bernensia*, the "foolish Amintas"
of *Eclogue* II, 39 is none other than Cornificius.

[2] *Ecl.* IX, 35: "neque adhuc Vario videor nec dicere Cinna
digna."

[3] They called him the Latin Siren, the only one who knew
how to read (i.e. declaim) poets and how to make them. Thus
runs an epigram of Furius Bibaculus (Suedonius, *De Gram-
maticis et Rhetoribus*, II).

[4] Cartault, p. 20; Schanz, II, I³, § 216; Catullus, XII, 6 ff.

[5] Cartault, p. 42.

that he very early came under the influence of the
new school, and that his initial essays profited by
his familiarity with the Alexandrine poets.

More than this we do not know. We know
neither how long Virgil stayed in Rome, nor when
he returned to the place of his birth, nor whether
his Roman sojourn was, as is probable, interrupted
by visits to his family. The years of civil war could
not have been, even for a friend of Caesar's, propitious for the serene culture of the Muses in Rome;
it is not improbable that he early sought a tranquil refuge in the Mantuan country, where he had
passed the years of his boyhood and where the
storm of fraternal discord had not yet broken
forth; for it was here, indeed, in that busy repose
amid country scenes, beside his well-known rivers
and sacred fountains, in the shade of his great oaks,
that he intoned the first songs on the humble pipes
of his shepherds.

II. Carmina Pastorum

SUMMARY: 1. The supposed juvenile works. — 2. The *Bucolics*. Events in the history of Rome before the composition of the *Bucolics*. Pollio and Virgil. — 3. *Alexis, Palaemon, Daphnis, Meliboeus*.

1

VIRGIL'S first essay in poetry was, according to Donatus, the epigram on the tomb of the robber Ballista:

Monte sub hoc lapidum tegitur Ballista sepultus;
    nocte die tutum carpe, viator, iter.

This Ballista was a school-master who had been guilty of petty thievery.[1] The distich is said to have been composed by Virgil when still a boy. This anecdote is appropriately embroidered by Focas in his poem. He asserts, without mentioning the studies of Virgil at Cremona and at Milan, that Ballista received the youth into his school at a time when he scarcely knew how to speak. By day the master taught his boys, by night he assailed his victims in the streets. When he was stoned to death and bur-

---

[1] Brummer, p. 4, l. 51: "poeticam puer adhuc auspicatus in Ballistam, ludi magistrum, ob infamiam latrociniorum coopertum lapidibus, disticon fecit." The Vulgate recension, to be sure, calls him a trainer of gladiators: "*ludi gladiatorii magistrum.*"Servius (Brummer, p. 69, l. 10) says simply "a robber."

42

ied under a heap of rocks, his pupil composed his epitaph.[1] One need hardly add that this epitaph was probably one of the exercises customary in grammar schools at the Poet's time. If the attribution to Virgil is really attested by Suetonius, there are grounds for accepting it. But does that settle the case?

Poems of so fine and delicate a structure as the *Bucolics* presuppose a long novitiate in the art of poetry. In truth Virgil had served his apprenticeship; before writing the *Eclogues* he too had practised the imitation of Greek models, or had taken daring little flights to strengthen the wings of his fantasy. The biographers attribute to the Poet's youth seven or eight minor works, with the particular intent of showing his precocious genius. These juvenile works were, according to Donatus and Servius, the *Catalepton*, the *Priapea*, the *Epigrammata*, the *Ciris*, the *Copa*, the *Dirae*, the *Culex*, and the *Aetna*.[2] Servius does not tell us at what age Virgil wrote these little poems; he contents himself with placing them before the *Bucolics*. On the other

---

[1] Brummer, p. 51, ll. 65–72.

[2] Donatus (Brummer, pp. 4–5): "deinde catalecton et priapea et epigrammata et diras, item cirim < et copam > (Bährens) et culicem, cum esset annorum XXVI ... scripsit etiam, de qua ambigitur, aetnam." The number XXVI is a conjecture of Scaliger, accepted also by Vollmer. The more authoritative manuscripts have XVI, one only has XVII, and two XV. The change to XXVI was suggested by a passage in Statius, *Silvae*, II, 7, 73. For Servius, cf. Brummer, p. 69.

hand, the manuscripts of Donatus seem to fix their composition at the time when Virgil was between fifteen and seventeen. I say "seem" for the following reason. The two manuscripts of London and of Brussels, which Brummer considers to be extracts from the *Life* by Donatus, make mention only of the *Culex*, which was written when the Poet was sixteen years of age.[1] Nor does Focas, who is supposed, I know not why, to depend on Donatus, recognize any other juvenile works except the *Culex*, written before the young Poet went to Rome.[2] The "sixteen years" of the other Donatian manuscripts might, then, refer only to the *Culex* and not to the whole collection mentioned by Donatus.

It is difficult to ascertain just when the first collection of the so-called juvenile works of Virgil was formed. It is generally held that the writings above mentioned, except the *Copa*, already formed a complete *Corpus* in the time of Suetonius, upon whom, it is claimed, Donatus entirely depends. This is one conjecture based upon another conjecture. In default of reliable information, the confusion of the hypotheses advanced is so great as to leave no hope of arriving at any degree of certainty. One thing is clear, that there is no mention of the early poems either in Ovid, or in Propertius, or in

[1] Brummer, p. 4, l. 67: "fecit et culicem cum esset annorum XVI."

[2] Brummer, p. 52, l. 84.

any of the writers of the time of Augustus, who
very often allude to the *Bucolics*, to the *Georgics*,
and to the *Aeneid*, and, what is still more strange,
that Macrobius seems to be entirely ignorant of
them, though he is the foremost authority on Virgil next to Servius.[1] The first sure reference to the
Culex is a phrase of Lucan's, to which Suetonius refers.[2] Further, the two well-known passages in the
Silvae of Statius concern only the *Culex*, which the
poet implies was not written before Virgil had attained the age of twenty-six.[3] Statius recalls this
little poem to remark upon its rather humble style
and to observe that it bears the same relation to
the *Aeneid* as the *Batrachomyamachia* to the *Iliad*.
The same idea is expressed by Martial,[4] for he too
contrasts the roughness of the *Culex* with the finish
of the epic poem. Quintilian[5] is ready to accept
as authentic the second epigram of the *Catalepton*.
This is all that the writers of the first century have
transmitted to us about the juvenile works cata-
logued by Donatus and by Servius; to tell the truth,
it is not much. Unless we would lose ourselves in
baseless suppositions, as do Vollmer and many
others who believe in the authenticity of all the

[1] Macrobius, *Saturnalia*, V, 17, 20: "Omnia opera sua Graece
maluit inscribere: *Bucolica, Georgica, Aeneis.*"

[2] *Vita Lucani* (ed. Reifferscheid), p. 50.

[3] *Silvae, praef, lib.* I; II, 7, 73.

[4] *Epigr.*, VIII, 55 (56), 19: "Protinus ITALIAM concepit et
ARMA VIRUMQUE, | qui modo vix Culicem fleverat ore rudi."

[5] *Inst. Or.*, VIII, 3, 27 f.

minor poems, we must content ourselves with asserting that only in the time of Servius do we find indubitable evidence of the existence of the collection that, by hypothesis, goes back to the time of Lucius Varius, and beyond. Besides, the list of Servius did not remain closed; other little poems, particularly the *Moretum,* were added to it at various times in the Middle Ages.

If, putting aside the testimony of the grammarians and the bibliographers, we ask ourselves what is truly Virgilian in the minor poems, we may admit that some of them, like the *Copa* and the *Moretum,* are in quality not unworthy of the poet of the *Bucolics;* the *Culex,* too, that academic imitation of a Greek original, might not be unsuited to him. Almost all the other pieces, however, are little in accord with the established conception of Virgil, except perhaps some pretty little bits from the *Catalepton.* But this acknowledgment does not authorize us, without any other proof, to consider as Virgilian poems which have only a certain Virgilian savor that might be caught in an imitation. It is more probable, in my opinion, that authenticity may be claimed for certain epigrams of the *Catalepton,* into which, together with compositions reflecting circumstances in the life of our Poet and of his friends, have crept others that are spurious. The genuine poems, *vers d'occasion,* might have circulated among the friends of the Poet and then have been inserted in collections of little pieces of the same sort.

In any event, one thing seems certain, that even those minor poems that have the greater likelihood of authenticity did not see the light before the death of Virgil, who had, as we know, the scruples of a delicate artist. If he did not publish them, that means he did not consider them worthy, and so they remained for him virtually non-existent. Nor, in case they should be proved sure products of his genius, would his poetic glory be thereby increased; at the most, they might serve as evidence for clearing up obscure points in his life and explaining the evolution of his art.

2

THE first work which Virgil signed with his name of poet was without doubt the *Bucolics*. Donatus informs us that, before putting hand to this form of verse, he had ventured an epic, taking as his subject the deeds of the Romans, — perhaps following the example of Ennius, — but that, finding the matter too difficult, he had dropped it and turned to pastoral poetry.[1] This statement probably has no other source than some ancient gloss on verses 3–5 of *Eclogue* VI:

[1] Brummer, p. 5, l. 65: "Mox cum res Romanas inchoasset, offensus materia ad bucolica transit."

> Cum canerem reges et proelia, Cynthius aurem
> vellit et admonuit: "pastorem, Tityre, pinguis
> pascere oportet ovis, deductum dicere carmen."

What kings and what battles Virgil had begun to
sing when still a youth, was not known to the ancient commentators, as we can see from their dis-
cordant glosses.[1] Nor is it safe to guess that the
plucking of the Poet's ear by Apollo is a kindly
allusion to the counsel given by some authoritative
friend, which to the Poet amounted to a command.
It is thought that the exhortation to dedicate himself to the bucolic type of poetry came from Asinius
Pollio, whose praises the Poet sounds.[2] This conjecture is founded on the *iussis carmina coepta tuis*
of the *Eighth Eclogue*,[3] dedicated to Pollio, and it is
made to apply to the entire work.

According to a statement worthy of attention, apparently supported by the authority of the learned
Asconius Pedianus, born scarcely twenty years after
the death of the Poet, Virgil set about writing the

[1] Servius, on *Ecl.* VI, 3, comments: "Et significat Aeneidem,
aut gesta regum Albanorum, quae coepta omisit, nominum as-
peritate deterritus." So also Philargyrius, and the Berne Scholia, on *Ecl.* VI, 3. Somewhat different is the gloss of Servius
Danielis. Cf. Vollmer, *Rhein. Mus.*, LXI (1906), 484; Funaioli,
Riv. Filol. Istr. Class, XLVII (1919), 382 ff.

[2] Servius (Brummer, p. 70, 1. 23): "Ei proposuit Pollio ut
carmen bucolicum scriberet, quod eum constat triennio scrip-
sisse et emendasse." See also the Bodleian manuscript of Donatus (Brummer, p. 25).

[3] Ll. 11–12. Cf. also *Ecl.* III, 84, 86.

Bucolics at the age of twenty-eight[1] and brought
the work to an end in three years.[2] Since he became twenty-eight years of age on the 15th of October, 42 B.C., the *Bucolics* would have been composed between the end of 42 and the end of 39.
This date is generally accepted by those versed in
Virgilian affairs, save for a broad interpretation of
the period of three years.

Although the pastoral songs of the Mantuan Poet,
according to Virgil's own confession, are inspired
by an Alexandrian model, the *Idylls* of Theocritus,
— and indeed they contain frequent imitations of
the Syracusan poet, — still they reflect both natural and historical reality; at times we see the bare
Mantuan landscape, however transfigured by Theocritean color, and amid the rustling of the leaves
and the sound of the pipes, we hear a distant rum-
bling of arms and the echo of the trumpet of war.
Nor would it be easy to understand the frequent
allusions to deeds and persons without knowledge
of the historic events of which the Poet was a spec-
tator and, for the moment, a victim.

[1] Probus, *Vita* (Brummer, p. 73, l. 12): "Scripsit Bucolica
annos natus VIII et XX Theocritum secutus." Probus, *Ecl.
praef.* (Thilo and Hagen, III, 2, 329): "Cum certum sit eum, ut
Asconius Pedianus dicit, XXVIII annos natum bucolica edi-
disse." Cf. Servius, *Ecl. praef.* (Thilo and Hagen, III, 1, p. 3):
Scholia Bernensia on *Georg.* IV, 565.

[2] Donatus (Brummer, p. 6, l. 89): "Bucolica triennio . . .
perfecit." Cf. Servius (*Ibid.*, p. 70, l. 24): Focas (*Ibid.*, p. 53,
l. 119).

Four years of civil war (49–45) had assured to
Julius Caesar the absolute control of the state. He
had rid himself of his more powerful enemy by his
presence of mind, by his perfect self-mastery even
in the most hazardous attempts, and by his power
of will, which he knew how to infuse into the minds
of his soldiers. After he had settled his great account with Pompey at Pharsalus, he pursued the
Pompeian forces into Egypt. There he suppressed
an attempt at revolt, and, without wasting any
time, he turned toward the East where the son of
Mithradates, profiting by the civil war, had taken
up arms to reconquer a part of the paternal king-
dom. Caesar defeated him in a single battle, and
announced his victory to the Senate in the famous
dispatch conceived in the style of an heraldic device: "I came, I saw, I conquered."

Although he was acclaimed by the people dictator for one year, and tribune for all time, he did not
repose on his laurels. A new gigantic struggle
awaited him in Africa. After the murder of Pompey, the Pompeians had concentrated in Mauri-
tania and had won over King Juba from their opponents' side. These must be subdued. In the
middle of the winter of 46, Caesar set out for Africa
with his legions, and in the spring conquered Publius Scipio at Thapsus; then, when he had put Juba
and Afranius to rout, he turned toward Utica,
where Marcus Cato was, hoping to capture him

alive. But the ancient and unconquerable enemy of Caesar preferred death by his own hand, and his example was followed by other chiefs of the Pompeian party.

After his victory in Africa, the great captain returned to Rome amidst the acclamations of an exultant people. After a *supplicatio* of forty days had been decreed in his honor, four triumphs were granted him, — over Gaul, over Egypt, over Pontus, and over Africa, — which are described by the Roman historians with great wealth of detail. The Senate then conferred the dictatorship on him for ten years.

But not even then was Caesar permitted to rest. Sextus Pompey, the son of Caesar's great adversary, taking the remainder of the African army, had aroused a large part of Farther Spain to rebellion. Caesar left Rome in the heart of winter and in twenty-seven days reached the scene of the new war. With the victory of Munda in March, 45, the last Pompeian forces were exhausted. The civil war might be called finished. The Senate decreed to the conqueror the honors of a fifth triumph and a *supplicatio* of fifty days; they conferred upon him the permanent dictatorship, and bestowed upon him the titles of *pater patriae*, of *imperator*, and of *sacrosanctus*. The title of *imperator*, "commander," which up to now had been the honorary title of a general who had brought an enterprise to a happy terminus, was applied to one who had gained supreme authority in the state. That meant monarchy; antiquity was not wrong in regarding Caesar as the first Roman emperor.

Once master of the Roman world, Caesar was faced with a new task. He had already shown great ability and exquisite tact as a statesman, no less than excellence as a leader, in his government of the Gallic provinces. Above all, he had succeeded in pacifying the peoples recently subdued. Now with quick wit, with a perfect grasp of the needs of Italy and with a sense of equity unmarred by base rancor, he devoted himself to the re-establishment of order and to the reform of both civic and municipal administration on the basis of a greater justice, guaranteed by a severe and prompt control. Rome was rid of all its former demagogues and of its idlers. Lands were distributed and colonists were sent to the provinces beyond the sea. Life became normal again, and the fields, made fecund by tranquil labor, smiled with renewed fertility.

Virgil was twenty-six years old when the life of Caesar was suddenly cut short, on the Ides of March, 44 B.C., just when he was preparing to go to war against the Parthians to vindicate the national shame caused by the defeat of Crassus and to put an end, once for all, to the attempts at invasion that threatened Syria. The preparations for the expedition were now finished. With the legions concentrated at Apollonia, in Epirus, was Octavius, a lad scarcely nineteen years of age, the son of Caesar's niece, Atia, and of C. Octavian. The young warrior was to accompany his uncle to learn, under the guidance of that great master, how to govern the world.

If the assassination and sudden disappearance of Caesar in the full glory of his activity as legislator threw his partisans into a panic, it likewise produced a certain bewilderment in the minds of his adversaries. These latter had agreed on the suppression of the dictator, but not on the course of action next to pursue. Mark Antony, a colleague of Caesar's in the consulate, took into his own hands the reins of government, imagining that he could replace the great departed and, with the support of Lepidus, assume the political succession. Meanwhile, under the protection of the Senate, the conspirators had succeeded in escaping from Rome unscathed, and thus some of them could return to govern the provinces to which they had been assigned by the man whom they had assassinated. Among these was Decimus Brutus, who had received from Caesar the command of Cisalpine Gaul.

For the success of his plans, Antony had first to get rid of the chiefs of the conspiracy, averse to Caesar's party, without, however, antagonizing the Senate, which desired a general reconciliation instead of civil war. Besides, he must see that a dangerous rival, the young Octavius, should not rise against him to claim the succession of his great-uncle. Now, while Antony was inciting the people to avenge the assassination and was gradually incurring the enmity of the Senate, Octavius hastened from Apollonia to Rome, and, presenting himself to the consul, asked that the will should be respected, wherein Caesar had made him heir to half his possessions, calling him his adopted son, with the right to assume his name. As soon as Antony refused to recognize the adoption, Octavius cleverly put himself on the side of the Senate, showing the greatest deference towards the deliberations of the conscript fathers; in the meantime he sought to gain the favor of the people and the good will of Caesar's veterans. He succeeded so well that very soon two legions abandoned Antony, and went over to him.

Again they were plunged in civil war. As soon as Antony had regained his strength, he moved against Decimus Brutus, who had fortified himself in Modena; the Senate exhorted Brutus to resistance and declared war on Antony, sending out against him the two consuls of the year 43, Vibius Pansa and Hirtius. The young Octavius then declared himself against Antony and in favor of the Senate, and henceforth he assumed the name of Iulius Caesar Octavianus. Besides the name, he had inherited from his adopted father the sympathy and the good wishes of the people and of the veterans. He had at his command a force considerably stronger than that of the consuls. To flatter him, the Senate nominated him senator, in spite of his not being of legal age.

In the spring of 43, in the plain between Modena and Bologna, a fierce struggle was waged. Of the two consuls, Hirtius died in battle and Vibius Pansa shortly afterwards from severe wounds. But Antony was conquered and was constrained to seek refuge with Lepidus, proconsul of Gallia Narbonensis. The fruits of the victory, however, were destined to fall, not to the senatorial party, but to Octavian, who, it was said, had not even taken part in the battle of Modena, and was actually accused of the deaths of the consuls. Inasmuch as the Senate decreed great honors on Decimus Brutus, and seemed to take no heed of Octavian, the latter went before them and requested that he succeed one of the slain consuls. The Senate did not grant the demand, but conceded to him only the right to present his candidacy when he should have attained the age of twenty. Octavian, indignant, made a pact with Antony and with Lepidus; moving with his legions against Rome, he assumed the consulship by main force, with Quintus Pedius as his colleague, whom Caesar had named as heir to a fourth part of the estate.

Once consul, he could think of avenging the

death of Caesar and of satisfying the impatient desires of the veterans. Planning an attack against Brutus and Cassius, who with the consent of the Senate were maintaining their commands in the East, he met Antony and Lepidus at a place somewhere between Modena and Bologna, and when they had come to an agreement, he proclaimed a triumvirate for a period of five years (from the 27th of November, 43, to the end of 49) with full powers to reorganize the state. On the basis of this agreement, the command of Spain and of Gallia Narbonensis was assigned to Lepidus; to Antony were given the other Gallic provinces, while to Octavian fell the command of Africa, with that of Sardinia and of Sicily. But this latter island was firmly held by Sextus Pompey who, with his fleet, dominated all the surrounding sea. Antony sent as his lieutenant into Cisalpine Gaul, C. Asinius Pollio, whose name will resound many times, as we shall see, in the pastoral songs of Virgil.

Taking advantage of their full powers, the triumvirate began to reorganize public offices, ejecting all the partisans of the Senate, and publishing long lists of proscriptions and confiscations. Numerous equites were proscribed and fully 130 senators. Cicero, the fiercest enemy of Antony, was ordered to be decapitated, at sixty-three years of age, by the legionary Popilius; his head and his right hand were exposed on the Rostra. Other capital punishments were ordered and quickly executed.

In the midst of these events there took place the apotheosis of Julius Caesar. It was probably in July, 43, on the occasion of the dedication of a temple to Venus Genetrix that Octavian instituted the funeral games in honor of his adopted father. During these games a comet appeared in the sky. The belief of the ancients in these celestial signs is well known. The apparition made a profound impression on the people, who held their slain leader in affectionate veneration. The report circulated that this was the soul of Caesar, received into the sky, and it was called the star of Caesar.[1] Octavian noted the event in his *Memoirs* and he had a golden star placed on the head of his father's statue which had been set up in the forum.[2] At the end of the same year, or rather in January, 42 B.C., the triumvirs bestowed divine honors upon Caesar, and on the Kalends of the same month they took oath on the acts of the god. Octavian, who through testamentary rights had assumed the name of his adopted father, began to call himself *divi filius*, son of the Divine. It was held by some ancient commentators that Virgil dedicated one of his most beautiful eclogues, *Daphnis*, to the Apotheosis of Caesar.

[1] Virgil, *Ecl.* IX, 47: "Ecce Dionaei processit Caesaris astrum." Cf. Suetonius, *Iul. Caes.*, 88.

[2] Cartault, pp. 17 f.

3

IN THE tangled chronological skein of Virgil's bucolic poems, there are certain points that we should clear up at the start. The first is that the order in which they were published does not exactly correspond to the order of their composition.[1] The second is that the *Eclogues* IV and VIII are dated, the one referring to the consulship of Pollio,[2] and the other to the war against the Parthini.[3] It is certain, moreover, that the second and third eclogues precede the fifth, and that the tenth is the last composed.[4] On these four points there is no essential disagreement among students of the *Bucolics*. All else, however, is matter for discussion, and discussion has been carried on by scholars with copious erudition and a diverse array of conjectures.

Without entering into the *selva selvaggia* of controversy, we shall limit ourselves to a survey of the most probable order of the pastoral poems in relation to the development of Virgil's art.

One sure point, as we have already observed, is that the second and third eclogues precede the fifth;

[1] "Bucolica scripsit, sed non eodem ordine edidit, quo scripsit" (Probus, *Praef. ad Buc.*, Thilo and Hagen, III, 2, p. 328). "De eclogis multi dubitant, quae licet decem sint, incertum tamen est, quo ordine scriptae sint" (Servius, *Praef. ad Buc.*, Thilo and Hagen, III, 1, p. 3).

[2] Cf. *Ecl.* IV, 3, 11.

[3] Cf. *Ecl.* VIII, 6–7, 13.

[4] *Ecl.* X, 1: "Extremum hunc, Arethusa, mihi concede laborem."

but this last, *Daphnis*, is not dated. Besides, by a
not altogether absurd conjecture, of which we shall
speak later, it is said to allude to the apotheosis of
Julius Caesar. Some, like Martin, have thought
they could confidently assign it to the year 42 B.C.,
but, as Heyne notes, even if we admit that in *Daphnis* Virgil intends to sing of Caesar, it does not nec-
essarily follow that he wrote it in the same year in
which divine honors were attributed to the Dictator; he might well have profited by some later occasion, at some annual celebration instituted in his
honor. There is, then, no sure conclusion as to date
to be drawn from this poem. On the other hand, in
the *Third Eclogue*, there is an important clue in the
passage where the two shepherds compete in their
praises of Pollio.

We have already mentioned C. Asinius Pollio
among the young poets and men of letters of the
new school at the time of Virgil's first sojourn at
Rome.[1] At the out break of the civil war between
Caesar and Pompey, Pollio was of the party of
Caesar. Not only did Caesar demand his presence
when he crossed the Rubicon, but he sent him afterwards to the command of Sicily, in the place of
Cato, who rejoined Pompey. And although Caesar's commentaries on the civil war have nothing
to say about Pollio, we know, nevertheless, that he
took part in the battle of Pharsalus, after which he

[1] See above, p. 40.

returned to Rome in company with Mark Antony, whose devoted friend and servant he was. He then followed Caesar to Africa and fought at Thapsus. When he returned again to Rome in 45 B.C. Caesar gave him the praetorship. He had already departed from Rome when the conspirators killed the Dictator. He then was in command in Farther Spain. From a letter of his sent to Cicero in 43, we find that he was a friend of Cornelius Gallus, who in his turn was friend and fellow-pupil of Virgil, and that in the midst of political and military occupations he found time to think about letters. At the end of this same year, when the Second Triumvirate was concluded, Antony recompensed him by entrusting him with the government of Cisalpine Gaul, which he held probably until 40 B.C., in which year he obtained the consulate. The anecdote told by Macrobius seems to refer to this period, and admirably characterizes the man and the moment.[1] When the triumvir Octavian satirized Pollio, friend of Antony, in Fescennine verses, the governor of Cisalpine Gaul contented himself with observing: "'Tis well to be silent; for it does not pay to describe one who might proscribe."

It is not possible to determine with certainty just when Virgil gained the friendship of Pollio. He certainly knew him when he was governing the Cisalpine district if not before — and he might well

[1] *Saturnalia*, II, 4.

have met him in Rome, on some one of the occasions when the friend of Caesar and of Antony appeared there after Pharsalus and after the compaign in Africa. The allusion to Pollio in the *Third Eclogue* shows us that he was pleased with Virgil's pastoral poems, which Servius would have us believe were written at his command. Virgil also calls him his reader.[1] What other Virgilian songs, we wonder, had Pollio praised besides the *Second Eclogue?*

The first bucolic poem, then, in the order of composition would appear to be *Alexis*, which together with *Palaemon* and *Daphnis*, and with *Meliboeus*, which is closely related to these, would seem to belong to the period in which Pollio remained in Cisalpine Gaul.

Alexis is the lament of a rich shepherd, Corydon, who is smitten with the lovely Alexis, Alexis pays no heed to his gifts nor to his mastery of song, and despises him because he is a coarse farmer, preferring Iollas to him. The song is of purely Theocritean inspiration. Heyne is not wrong in finding it less beautiful than the others, though admitting its notable artistic technique and excellence of form — a judgment with which the commentators in general agree.

The theme of the eclogue seems early to have

---

[1] *Ecl.* III, 84: "Pollio amat nostram, quamvis est rustica, Musam. |Pierides, vitulam lectori pascito vestro."

called forth sarcasms from evil-minded critics, well
disposed to place credence in the commentators and
their array of silly gossip concerning the Poet. It
is related that Virgil, at a supper to which he was
invited by Pollio, admired a beautiful slave, Alexander by name, whom the governor of Gaul wished
to bestow on him. The idea of the poem *Alexis*,
then, originated in the love that Virgil had for this
slave.[1] But this story, even if it be true, does not, as
it is claimed, explain Virgil's meaning, with which
it has not the slightest connection. Virgil meant,
rather, merely to vary the theme of the pseudo-
Theocritean Idyll XXIII, where a lover, smitten
with longing for a cruel youth, hangs himself at the
loved one's door. On no other foundation than the
allegorical interpretation of this eclogue and the
attribution of *Catalepton* VII (IX) to Virgil, we are
asked to believe what the commentators, perhaps
depicting themselves a little, have to say about his
predilection for boys.

The structure of this first bucolic poem reveals a
fundamental characteristic of all Virgil's poetry —
high originality despite the imitation of the Greek

[1] Donatus (Brummer, p. 3, ll. 28–31): "Libidinis in pueros
pronioris, quorum maxime dilexit Cebetem et Alexandrum,
quem secunda bucolicorum ecloga Alexim appellat, donatum
sibi ab Asinio Polione, utrumque non ineruditum, Cebetem
vero et poetam." Cf. Servius, on *Ecl.* II, 1, 15. See also the
note of Heyne on the *Life* by Donatus, § 20; Pascal, *op. cit.*,
pp. 22 ff. Diehl, p. 11: Funaioli, *Allegorie Virgiliane*, in *Ras-
segna ital. lingue e letter. class.*, II (1920), 166 ff.

models. In *Alexis* the Poet plunders Theocritus outright. However, the eclogue has an inner unity all its own and entirely new; the numerous reminiscences of Theocritus that commentators have discovered stand out rather as unpolished material than as constituent elements of the poem. All this, as Albini has seen better than anyone else, is an "artistic divagation," a music of fine verses, which a shepherd enamored of song, rather than of Alexis, tosses to the mountains and the woods from the pure need of singing. Virgil's shepherds are all lovers of song, and song resounds in all his pastoral scenes.

The *Third Eclogue, Palaemon*, presents a contest of shepherds who challenge each other to song after having exchanged not a few gross ribaldries. The alternating songs that "please the Muses" put an end to the mutual abuse. Palaemon, who by chance passes by, is judge of the contest. But more than judge and critic, he is a listener, who admires and enjoys the bravura of the singers. At the end he declares himself incapable of deciding which of the two has surpassed his rival, — because, he says, whoever confides to song what has been inspired by love through either hope or suffering, is a true poet and merits the prize.

Palaemon also is imitated from Theocritus, except the close; but you already feel that the landscape which serves as background to the pastoral

scene is inspired by the Mantuan country, especially in the last verse:

Close the sluices, lads; the fields have drunk their fill.

With this touch of Cisalpine landscape, the Poet
makes a neat bow to Pollio, friend of the pastoral
muses, and himself a maker of new songs; it is also
a chastisement of Bavius and Maevius, whose names
give us a glimpse of the literary quarrels in Rome
and add a vivacious tone to the song of the two
shepherds.

Third in order of time comes the *Fifth Eclogue,
Daphnis.* While the preceding poem begins with a
vivacious exchange of insults between the two rival
shepherds, this one opens, as is suitable to the subject, with a courteous invitation, which Menalcas,
a shepherd-poet, extends to another shepherd, his
friend Mopsus, also skilled with the pipes, to while
away the time with him in song. Mopsus accepts
the welcome proposal and points out a grotto,
clothed with festoons of wild vines, where they can
lie in the shade. There is just a flaunt at Amyntas,
a good player on the pipes, but so full of vanity that
he would challenge Apollo himself — and then the
shepherds exchange their gifts of their song.

Mopsus, first, intones the verses which he had
just cut on the bark of a beech-tree, setting them to
music note by note. He sings of the plaint of the
nymphs for Daphnis, his life extinguished by a cruel

death, while, clasping her son's wretched corpse, his mother calls on the gods and stars that pity not; the anguish of the shepherds penetrates their cattle, and the moaning of wild beasts is heard, and the heartbroken echo of the mountains and the woods. Then after praising the dead shepherd, he turns again to depict the desolation of the fields, and calls for funeral honors such as would be suitable for the "more beautiful guardian of a beautiful herd." The song of Mopsus soothes the ravished soul of Menalcas as the weary are soothed by sleep on the grass, as thirst in summer's heat is quenched by a gushing rivulet of sweet water.

The song of Mopsus is fine and tender; more robust and elevated, almost epic, is that of Menalcas. Daphnis, once guardian of the sylvan herd, now radiantly touches the threshold of Olympus and sees the clouds and stars beneath his feet. Gay pleasure animates the woods and all the countryside; gay are Pan and the shepherds and the Dryad maidens; the flock fears not the ambush of the wolves, nor the deer the nets of the hunter; gentle Daphnis again bestows peace upon the renovated land; the wooded mountains and the very rocks, the very copses repeat the song: "A god, a god is he, O Menalcas!" The new god is invoked by the shepherd. To him and to Phoebus altars are erected, libations are offered, and with song and dance their vows are made, as to Bacchus and Ceres.

At the end of the eclogue, the two singers exchange gifts. Suddenly Menalcas reveals himself as none other than Virgil, whose fragile pipes had inspired the lament of Corydon for the beautiful Alexis, and the poetic debate of *Palaemon*.

In this beautiful poem we again find imitations of Theocritean idylls placed in relief, especially in the song of the first shepherd where he mourns the death of Daphnis. But one must recognize that Virgil takes not a little liberty with his Greek model, and that the imitation almost entirely disappears in the song of Menalcas, which is the true novelty in Virgil's poem. The apotheosis, which here is the culminating point, is lacking not only in Theocritus but in all other versions of the legend of Daphnis, although in some of them he is translated to the skies, in pity, by his father Hermes. For this is the essential difference between Virgil's Daphnis and the *First Idyll* of Theocritus, as Cartault has well noted:[1] while Theocritus concerns himself with the death of the Sicilian shepherd and with his suffering, spent as he was with consuming love, Virgil begins his song with the plaint of the Nymphs and with the grief of the mother, who holds in her arms the lifeless body of her son, cruelly slain; all that follows is meant to be a continuation rather than an imitation of the song of Theocritus.

Further, the lament is specifically Roman. In

[1] *Op. cit.*, p. 166.

the cult rendered to the new god, there is a fleeting
suggestion of the Ambarvalian rites proper to the
Roman religion. And while there was still fresh the
memory of the recent murder of Caesar and of the
divine honors conferred on him by the triumvirs
and the people, how was it possible to write or to
read this song, as Albini justly remarks,[1] without
seeing the great shade of the Roman ruler set in
relief against the simple figure of Daphnis?

The ancient commentators have recorded many
different allegorical interpretations of this eclogue.
Some of them perceive in Daphnis, Julius Caesar;
others Flaccus, brother of Virgil; others Saloninus
son of Pollio; others, finally, Quintilius Varus.
Never content, they extend their researches in allegory beyond all limits of possibility.[2] Without
spending more time on this matter, let us note only
that, if there is a partial allegory, it can be applied
only to Julius Caesar, to whom alone could be applied the acclamation: *Deus, deus ille Menalca!*

The name of Daphnis, applied to a simple shepherd and having nothing to do with the Daphnis
whose praises are sung in the present eclogue, recurs also in *Eclogue* VII, *Meliboeus*. Like *Palaemon*,
this new bucolic poem is an *amoeboean* song, simple

[1] *I carmi bucolici di Virgilio* (Bologna: Zanichelli, 1899),
pp. xxvi ff. Albini clinches his thesis with a greater abundance
of observation in his beautiful introduction to the new version
of the *Bucolics* (Bologna: Zanichelli, 1926), pp. 16 ff.

[2] Cf. Funaioli, *Alleg. Virg.*, pp. 175 ff.

and graceful, of pure Theocritean inspiration. In
its structure and in some slight touches, it is closely
allied to the group of the three eclogues of which
we have spoken. Corydon is the skilful singer of
Eclogue II, to which he makes evident allusion in
verses 55–56:

at si formosus Alexis
montibus his abeat, videas et flumina sicca.

The landscape which is drawn in the background
of this pastoral scene is Mantuan. We see a great
whispering ilex by the waters of the Mincio, whose
banks are clothed in pliant reeds. Two shepherds
have collected in the shade their flocks of sheep and
of goats. Farther on, another goatherd, intent on
protecting the tender myrtle from the approach of
winter's cold, does not observe the flight of the male
of the flock. In the fields are grazing bullocks, who,
when they have eaten, wander down to the river to
drink. A slight buzzing from a bee-hive in a yeared
oak animates the little picture, sketched with such
freshness of color.

III. Paulo Maiora

SUMMARY: 1. The political events which precede the *Fourth Eclogue.* — 2. The song of civil peace: *Pollio.* — 3. Alfenus Varus and Silenus. The *Pharmaceutria.* — 4. The spoliation of the lands. *Tityrus* and *Moeris.* The exile.

1

IF WITH the song of Menalcas in *Daphnis*, Virgil elevated somewhat the tone of the simple pastoral song, he made a still higher flight in *Pollio* and *Silenus*.

Paulo maiora canamus. In this poem as in the others of which we shall speak, the Poet still lingered, in the manner of Theocritus, among woods and shepherds; but his art, now sure of itself, began to turn with freer inspiration toward a vaster horizon than that of Theocritus, and to image a more complex reality. Even if this had not happened, Virgil would still have remained the prince of Arcadians for all time.

When they had agreed on their shares in the administration, the triumvirs thought not only to get rid of their enemies in Italy, but to forestall the menacing plots directed against them in the East by Junius Brutus and Cassius. The victory of Philippi in the autumn of 42 B.C. rendered Octavian and Antony masters of the Roman world, which

they proceeded soon to divide. The success of their
arms owed much to the devotion of the soldiers to
whom, before the war, a solemn promise had been
made to give over the fertile territory of some of
the richest municipalities of Italy and to pay a sum
of five thousand drachmae per head. Antony had
left for Asia to get money; Octavian came into
Italy, where he proceeded to distribute the lands
among the veterans. The decree for the spoliation
of the old inhabitants was issued in the spring of
41, but its execution probably took some time and
had to undergo delay on account of the events
which followed.

Appian and Cassius Dio and Velleius give us a
lively picture of the insurrections to which the decree of spoliation gave rise. The consuls in that
year were Lucius Antony, brother of Mark Antony,
and Publius Servilius Vatia. Fulvia, the wife of
Mark Antony, began to meddle in the affairs of
state; she intrigued with her brother-in-law and,
showing disdain for his colleague, assumed the rôle
of female consul for herself. The pair profited by
the general confusion caused by the confiscation of
the lands. Fulvia pretended that a settlement was
to be deferred until the return of her husband from
the East, while Lucius spread rumors that Octavian proposed to expel all the inhabitants of Italy
from their homes; he was lavish with promises to
the despoiled colonists, and at the same time set

the dissatisfied veterans against Caesar, inviting them to follow him in the defence for their rights.

Thus a new conflict appeared upon the horizon. On one side, Lucius Antony, while collecting a strong army and preparing for war, complained that Octavian had not given to him that part of the lands which belonged to the veterans of his brother; the triumvir, for his part, was incensed that the consul had deprived him of part of his army. The intriguing wife of Mark Antony fanned the flame. When Caesar tried to suppress an insurrection that broke out against him, civil war burst forth in fury. Driven from Rome, Lucius and Fulvia directed their steps toward Gaul, which was governed by the Antonian Pollio; but Caesar followed them there, and having caught up with them, besieged them in Perugia. In vain did Pollio with Ventidius and Munatius Plancus twice attempt to come to their aid; he was obliged both times to return to his province.

At the beginning of 40 B.C., according to the agreement reached by the triumvirs for the assignments of the offices, Asinius Pollio assumed the consulship with Cn. Domitius Calvinus. At the end of winter the besieged of Perugia were constrained to surrender. A generous pardon was conceded to Lucius. It is said, however, that not a few of his partisans, both equites and senators were sacrificed on the altar of Caesar.

Meanwhile Fulvia fled with her sons to her husband, inciting him to take arms against Octavian.
The latter, without losing any time, undertook to
follow the lieutenants of Antony into Gaul, to drive
them from their commands. Pollio was able to save
Venetia, gaining several victories, while the rest
of Northern Italy was occupied by the legions of
Salvidienus.

The events in Italy induced Mark Antony to
leave Egypt as soon as possible, where he was at the
time. After he had landed in Apulia, he occupied
Sepuntum and after a short time he overpowered
Brundisium, expelling Servilius Rullus, a general of
Octavian. To the young Horace in these years of
sad struggle, it seemed that Rome, unconquered by
the assaults of a hundred enemies, was now about
to fall by her own hand; with noble disdain, he exhorted good citizens, desirous of peace and a rem-
edy for their disasters, to abandon the Latin lands
which fraternal blood had stained, and to find a
tranquil refuge in the storied isles of the ocean.[1]

While Octavian was preparing to attach his colleague, now become his enemy, there came the news
of the death of Fulvia at Sicyon. To prevent further bloodshed and above all to appease the tired
veterans, who were demanding a truce and com-
pensations, Pollio and Maecenas and their common
friend, Lucius Cocceius, interposed their good of-

[1] Horace, *Epod.*, XVI.

fices between the two combatants, and at Brundisium itself, which had bade fair to become the
theatre of a new struggle, effected a reconciliation.
With the peace of Brundisium, the clouded political horizon became serene again, and those who,
like Horace, had longed for the return of peace,
could draw a long sigh of relief. The two triumvirs, settling their quarrels and donning their
triumphal robes, made their solemn entrance into
Rome amidst the exultations and plaudits of the
crowd.

The civil peace recently concluded, while it left
Octavian free to devote his attention to Sextus
Pompey, permitted Antony to settle affairs in the
Balkan Peninsula. The Parthinian tribes of Illyria,
who had openly favored Cassius, were now occupy-
ing the territory of Epidamnus. To reduce them to
obedience within their confines, Antony determined
to send against them a powerful expedition which
he entrusted to the command of his faithful lieutenant, Pollio. Pollio went off to the war towards
the end of autumn and at that time, by act of
surrogation, he was appointed consul. Since the
Fourth Eclogue refers explicitly to the consulate of
Pollio, there is no doubt that it was composed between the end of summer and the end of autumn of
40 B.C., that is, between the conclusion of the peace
of Brundisium and the departure of Pollio, to whom
it is dedicated.

2

To VIRGIL the peace of Brundisium seemed a prelude to a new era not only in the history of Rome
but in that of the world. The event happened to
coincide with a prophecy of the Sibylline songs,
widely diffused in popular belief. This ancient collection of oracles in charge of the *Quindecimviri*,
whose function was to consult and interpret them,
was destroyed in the burning of the Capitol, in
83 B.C. But the Senate had ordered the reconstruction of the books; this they accomplished by collecting all the Sibylline oracles of which traces could
be found in Italy and in the East. Thus it is probable that the new collection would include elements
of religious and philosophical Oriental doctrines,
especially Orphic and Heraclitean ideas propagated
along with Stoicism. According to these doctrines,
the life of the world describes a great circle; when
this is finished, there occurs a palingenesis, or a re-
birth of the universe. The duration of the great
year (*magnus annus*), as the cosmic cycle is called,
was calculated by the time it took the stars to return to their original position in respect to us; this
gave rise to astronomical calculations exceedingly
diverse. In the course of the world-cycles, the repe-
tition of the same events was also assured. The
great year was generally divided into ten great
months corresponding to the similar periods in

which the cycle of cosmic life was divided. The end of an age and the transition into a new one would be announced by some celestial miracle of which it was the signal (*signum*). Thus it is reported that the apparition of the comet during the funeral honors rendered to Caesar was interpreted by the soothsayer Vulcanius, or Vulcatius, to be the end of the ninth age and the beginning of the tenth.[1]

With these philosophic and religious doctrines it was sought to reconcile, in their essential ideas, the popular and poetic legend of the four ages of the world, named from the four metals, over each of which presided a god. We are not acquainted with the text of the Sibylline books mentioned by Virgil, nor do we know how much in them conforms to the collection which has come down to us. This at any rate Virgil thought he could read there: that the end of the last age of the world had now arrived, predicted by the oracle of the Cumaean Sibyl, and that the great cosmic year was about to begin again, together with the age of gold and the reign of Saturn:

> Ultima Cumaei venit iam carminis aetas;
>   magnus ab integro saeclorum nascitur ordo.

With the imminent cosmic regeneration was to begin a new era for humanity. The peace of Brun-

---

[1] Servius Danielis, on *Ecl.* IX, 46: "Vulcanius aruspex in contione dixit cometen esse, qui significaret exitum noni saeculi et ingressum decimi. . . . Hoc etiam Augustus in libro secundo de memoria vitae suae complexus est."

disium was a signal of its prelude. Pollio, who more
than any other had striven to effect a reconciliation,[1] could well boast that in his consulate the new
era of civil peace began, and that through his ef-
forts, the land, purified of all traces of its ancient
guilt, felt itself at last free from the fears which had
encumbered it without ceasing.

The *Pollio* is the song of civil peace. But in it
historical events are sublimated in an apocalyptic
light. Virgil's poem reflects the hope of a people,
who, freed from the suffering that had oppressed
them before, felt a keen joy after the long months
of anguish, and were lulled in the idyllic dream of
a blessed future. Towards that future the Poet's
fancy was impelled.

It was just at this time that a son was born, or
was about to be born, to Pollio.[2] Beside the cradle
of this scion of his friend and protector, Virgil
chants his song of peace.

The babe belongs to the new progeny of pure

[1] At the time of the battle of Mutina, he wrote from Cordova
to Cicero (March 16, 43 B.C.): "Natura autem mea et studia
trahunt me ad pacis et libertatis cupiditatem. Itaque illud
initium civilis belli saepe deflevi . . . Qua re eum me existima
esse, qui primum pacis cupidissimus sim (omnis enim civis
plane studeo esse salvos)," etc., Cicero, *Ad Fam.*, X, 31, 2–5.

[2] Servius Danielis, on *Ecl.* IV, II: "Quidam Saloninum Pollionis filium accipiunt, alii Asinium Gallum, fratrem Salonini,
qui prius natus est Pollione consule designato. Asconius Pedianus a Gallo audisse se refert, hanc eclogam in honorem eius
factam." For the other opinions of the commentators ancient
and modern cf. Cartault, pp. 227 ff., Schanz³, II, I, p. 48.

men who have descended from the ethereal mansions to inhabit the renovated earth; at his coming shall disappear the rude people of the iron age, while a golden race will be born into the world. The lad will live a life divine and will see the earth populated with heroes mingling with gods, and through the virtues of his father, he will govern a world at peace. The golden age, sung by the poet, the primal age of man, shall return; suffering and toil shall cease; justice and love shall reign among men without suspicion. Nature itself shall participate in this human regeneration. The serpent shall be no more; no more the poisonous grass; the untilled fields shall gradually grow white with the nodding lavender, the grape hang red from the wild briar, and the hardy oaks drip dew of honey...

The close of the poem is finely conceived and profoundly human. Though the description of the new age of gold has its commonplaces and the idea of the poem is somewhat rhetorical and Utopian, it admirably sets forth, with a magnificence of coloring, the aspirations of a world weary of struggle and the Poet's sure faith in the return of justice. Turning from his dream of the age to come, his fancy looks fondly on the little cradle by the side of which he has poured forth his song of peace. To the heaven-favored boy he expresses the kindly augury, which sums up the hope of his song:

Incipe, parve puer, risu cognoscere matrem.

In that first smile with which the babe recognizes the mother and compensates her for the nine long months of suffering, is the germ of all the joy which is to illuminate the world redeemed.

3

IF WITH *Pollio* Virgil breaks away completely from the imitation of Theocritus and turns his pastoral song to civic uses, he attempted still greater heights with *Silenus*, venturing a bucolical setting for philosophic ideas on the origin of the world.

The *Sixth Eclogue* is dedicated to Alfenus Varus, who was probably a fellow-pupil of Virgil in Rome at the school of Siro; he had possessions, so it seems, in Mantua.[1] After the surrender of Perugia, he succeeded Pollio in the government of the Transpadane country, from which the legate of Antony had been constrained to withdraw into Venetia.[2]

In the dedication of *Silenus* to Varus, Virgil excuses himself for not celebrating his exploits in war (his laurels were perhaps dripping with fraternal blood) since Apollo had admonished him, by twitching his ear, to content himself with pastoral

---

[1] Cf. above, p. 36, "Varus possessor mantuanus erat" (*Scholia Bernensia* on *Ecl.* VIII, 6).

[2] Servius Danielis, on *Ecl.* VI, 6: "Fugatoque Asinio Pollione, ab Augusto Alfenum Varum legatum substitutum, qui transpadanae provinciae et agris dividendis praeesset." Cf. on *Ecl.* IX, 27; *Scholia Bernensia*, on *Ecl.* VIII; 6; *Ecl. praef.* IX.

songs. The gentle Poet, who, no less than Pollio, abhorred the memory of the recent civil strife which had ensanguined Italian lands, could offer no better gift to the new ruler of his country than a song approved by Phoebus. We cannot believe that Virgil, dissatisfied with Varus, is merely seeking a pretext for not keeping his promise, made in another poem, to exalt his name to the stars.[1] For, waiving the supposition on which it rests, this explanation is immediately nullified when we consider the wish of the Poet that his humble song should cause the name of Varus to echo throughout the woods, and the kindly compliment that there is no page dearer to Phoebus than that which bears upon its top the name of Varus.[2] Worthy of note is the fact that, in this dedication there is lacking absolutely any hint at the measures taken by Alfenus Varus for the distribution of the Mantuan lands to the veterans, and particularly for Virgil's immunity from the confiscation of his property. This silence would indeed be inexplicable if the *Sixth Eclogue* followed the two eclogues that take their theme from the spoliation.

The poem that Virgil wished to be embellished with the name of Varus is one of the most beautiful of the collection. A delightful scene is depicted with spirit against the background of an Arcadian land-

---

[1] *Ecl.* IX, 27–29.
[2] Cf. Albini, *I carmi bucolici*, pp. xxxii f.

scape peopled with fauns, satyrs, nymphs, and
other rustic divinities, mingling with shepherds
and their flocks. Old Silenus occupies the centre of
the scene, the rural demi-god, the master and boon
companion of Bacchus. Chromis and Mnasyllus,
perhaps two fauns, perhaps two shepherds, surprise him stretched out in a grotto, heavy with
sleep, his veins swollen with the wine of yesterday.
There on the earth lay the garlands slid from his
head, and the wine-jar hanging from his hand by
its worn handle. They seize him and fetter him
with his own garlands, to keep him to his promise
of a song — for often he had disappointed them.
Aegle joins company and urges them on, Aegle the
fairest of the Naiads, and while the old fellow opens
his drowsy eyes, she stains his face with the juice
of mulberries. He, laughing at their wiles, with a
veiled threat for the fair nymph, begins to sing.
His harmonies possess the fauns and beasts, who
sport in measure, and the plants, whose crests
sway with rhythmic motion.

In this divine song of Silenus, the Poet merely
hints at the themes. The soul of the old satyr is an
inexhaustible source of poetry. Song follows song.
The birth of the world from the primal germs of
things, once chaotic in the infinite void, is sung
with slight hints of Lucretius.[1] Then come the

[1] On the Epicurean interpretation given to vv. 31-40 of this
eclogue is founded, as said above (p. 30), the statement that

myth of Pyrrha, the age of gold, the theft and the torture of Prometheus, the death of Hylas, and the bestial love of Pasiphae "for the snowy bull," then the story of Atalanta who marvelled at the golden apples of the Hesperides, and then the story of the sisters of Phaethon changed into alders, their bitter bark clothed with moss. One of Silenus's songs is dedicated to Cornelius Gallus, bound to Virgil by fraternal friendship as well as by the cult of the Muses. Gallus, so it seems, held at that moment an office in the Transpadane country[1] which was governed by Alfenus Varus; we shall see him, shortly, trying in vain to save Virgil from the spoliation of his lands. The praises offered to Varus in this song are not without intention on the part of the Poet. One of the Muses, sings Silenus, conducted Gallus to Helicon while he was wandering along the banks of the Permessus. Around him he perceived all the choir of Phoebus; Linus, the divine shepherd-singer, presented him in the name of the Muses with the pipes once given to Hesiod.[2]

Virgil attended the school of Siro; some ancient scholiasts would even discover Siro in Silenus. As a matter of fact, there is little Epicureanism in these verses; in spite of the reminiscences of the *De rerum natura* of Lucretius (shown by Cartault, pp. 269 ff.), the philosophy here set forth is equally near to that of Empedocles or even of Anaxagoras.

[1] Servius Danielis, on *Ecl.* VI, 64: "Qui [Gallus] a triumviris praepositus fuit ad exigendas pecunias ab his municipiis, quorum agri in Transpadana regione non dividebantur."

[2] The theory that Cornelius Gallus had introduced bucolic poetry into Latin before Virgil is asserted by Skutsch, *Gallus*

Still other songs the old singer rehearsed until
evening came and the shepherds led their flock to
the sheep-fold to tell their tale. The themes of these
songs are those of the Alexandrian school, which
inspired the young Latin poets derided by Cicero.
All the little streams of poetry, all the songs of
Apollo, says the Poet, that the river Eurotas heard
and its laurel-trees passed on, all these flowed together in a melodic wave that the singer poured
forth, inebriated with his song, as though beside
himself with Bacchic fury. If the inspiration of
Theocritus had sufficed Virgil in his first bucolic
poems, his poetical world had by this time noticeably broadened. Aratus, Euphorion, Apollonius of
Rhodes, Nicander, and others too, will have their
place in it; nor will Lucretius fail.

At the fall of evening, when the tireless singer
stops the flow of his song, the sky itself, "unwilling
Olympus," regrets the rising of the evening star.
Such imagery bespeaks a poet who has climbed
well up the slopes of Helicon.

The *Eighth Eclogue, Pharmaceutria,* was probably
written a little after *Silenus,* if not at the same time.
It contains, at any rate, sure indications of its
date. It is dedicated to Pollio, who had gone to
war against the Parthians toward the end of 40
B.C. After the capture of Salonae, in the following

und Vergil (Leipsic, 1906), pp. 128 ff. Cf. Schanz, II, I³, p. 209
(§271).

year, Antony's legate returned to Rome, laden with booty and with glory, and on the 25th of October he attained triumphal honors. When Virgil was at work on this eclogue, the news of Pollio's victories[1] had reached Italy, and it was known that he was on the way home; but he had not yet arrived there. Perhaps, as the Poet thinks, he was about to cross the Timavus, or he was skirting the coast of the Illyrian sea.[2] The dedication is, then, at the end of the summer or the beginning of the autumn of 39. The eclogue itself ought to be not much earlier, and, indeed, may not have been finished when the dedication was composed.

The *Pharmaceutria* is a return after *Pollio* and *Silenus* to pastoral song and the imitation of Theocritus. What more welcome gift could Virgil offer before Pollio, who had always encouraged him to cultivate the pastoral Muse? *Musam pastorum . . . dicemus* — these words, I think, were set at the beginning of the eclogue for the precise purpose of meeting his friend's wish, which for him was a command.[3] Nor was Pollio insensible to that sprig of ivy which the Poet would weave among the laurels

---

[1] Line 13 speaks of his "victorious laurels" (*inter victricis . . . lauros*). Cf. Sonntag, p. 89.

[2] Line 6:
"Seu magni superas iam saxa Timavi| sive oram Illyrici legis aequoris."
Cf. Cartault, pp. 299 f.

[3] Line 11:
"Accipe iussis|— carmina coepta tuis."

of victory that the conqueror of the Parthinians
awaited at Rome.

The eclogue is composed of two distinct songs,
freely imitated from Theocritus. At dawn Damon,
leaning against an olive-trunk, impersonates the
grief of a shepherd who has resolved to die because
his loved one has abandoned him to espouse another. Especially fine — and original — are the
verses that describe the bitter jealousy of the de-
ceived shepherd:

> Mopso Nysa datur: quid non speremus amantes? ...
> Mopse, novas incide faces: tibi ducitur uxor.
> sparge, marite, nuces: tibi deserit Hesperus Oetam!

So, too, the passage in which he recalls the moment when his love began, although it draws its
motive from the Syracusan poet, expresses a true
and delicate wistfulness and a true imprecation
against love:

> Through our own garden-close I guided thee,
> Thee a small maiden at thy mother's side,
> In search of dewy apples. My twelfth year
> Had scarce begun, yet standing on the ground
> I reached and broke the bending boughs for thee.
> I saw thee and was lost, blind, mad, a slave!

The song of the desperate shepherd finishes with
a farewell to the woods and with a renewed offering
of himself to death, not without the bitter thought
that his plunge into the waves will be a final gift
to her who had betrayed him.

In the answering song of Alphesiboeus, a woman
abandoned by her lover turns to magic arts to bring
him back to her. The imitation of Theocritus in
this second part of the eclogue assumes at times the
aspect of a translation, except that Virgil trans-
forms into lyric what in the Syracusan is a little
drama. The song of the sorceress, observes Cartault,[1] doubtless fascinated those ancient readers
who accepted magic rites as manifestations of some
irresistible and mysterious force. To us the song
of Alphesiboeus seems not so much an embodiment
of true poetry as a compound of elegant poetic de-
vices. There are some exceptions, such as the vow
of the sorceress that Daphnis shall be consumed
with love even as a mad heifer, who wearily seeks
her lost bullock through the deep thickets of the
grove. Neither the imagery nor the idea is found
in Theocritus; the imagery alone comes from Lucretius,[2] but Virgil adapts it to an idea of which
there is no trace in Lucretius.

The enchantments finally produce their effect.
The ashes that Amaryllis was to scatter in the river
shoot tremulous flames about the altar while she is
gathering them. Good augury, that; something is
about to happen; Hylax, the dog, is barking at the
door; Daphnis returns.

[1] *Op. cit.*, p. 313.
[2] II, 355 ff.

4

THE *Pharmaceutria* was to be the last poetical variation on a purely Theocritean theme in which Virgil indulged; it was a gift of reminiscence to his friend, as he returned in triumph from Illyria. From now on, stern reality was to inspire quite other pastoral songs.

We have already referred to the decree by which Octavian, on his return from Philippi in the spring of 41 B.C., distributed to the veterans the lands belonging to fully eighteen cities of Italy. We have also spoken of the consequent insurrections and of the opposition of Lucius Antonius to executing the Triumvir's order.[1] During the Perusine War, Pollio was governing the Cisalpine country; it is not likely that he would have wished to antagonize that district by carrying out a decree from Octavian, with whom he was in open warfare. In Cisalpine Gaul and especially in the Transpadane country, the occupation of the lands by the veterans could not have occurred except after the expulsion of Pollio from the government of Upper Italy. And this took place, as we know, after the fall of Perugia. Only then did the legions of Salvidienus enter the Cisalpine country, while Pollio offered a successful resistance in Venetia, near Altinum and at Padua. Even if Alfenus Varus and the other two triumvirs

[1] See above, p. 69.

appointed to measure off and assign the confiscated lands, had set to work immediately to satisfy the veterans, it is natural that the preliminary operations should have taken a certain length of time, and that this would not have begun simultaneously in all the cities of the region; it would also have proceeded in a certain order which depended on the favor and the assistance that the different cities had given to Antony's party during the preceding events. We know for a certainty that the territory of Cremona was invaded before that of Mantua because the inhabitants of that land had lent support to the enemies of Octavian. The Mantuan territory was occupied when it was seen that that of Cremona did not suffice. The nearness to Cremona accounted for Mantua's plight.[1] If such was the course of events, it is very probable that the invasion of Mantua did not take place before 39 B.C., and to this year must be assigned the two eclogues which deal with the spoliation, namely, *Tityrus* and *Moeris*.[2]

As soon as the decree of expropriation was extended to the Mantuan territory (not to all, it seems, but to just enough to satisfy the discontented veterans), the property of Virgil was found to be in the expropriated part, within the fifteen

[1] *Ecl.* IX, 28: "Mantua vae miserae nimium vicina Cremonae."

[2] For the evidence on this matter to be found in the ancient commentators, see below, Appendix II.

miles from the Cremona border.[1] Hence he lost it.
To retain it, he would have to secure an exception
to the decree, which Octavian alone could make.
To this end, he would have to go to Rome, where
with the support of influential friends, perhaps of
Gallus, he might be admitted to the presence of the
son of the divine Julius, and obtain from him the
restitution *de jure*, and the preservation *de facto*, of
his estate.[2] In the circumstances, would he also in-
tercede for his unfortunate compatriots? We do
not know; but we do know that this opinion is held
by several ancient commentators, as reported by
Servius.[3]

The first eclogue in the present order of the *Bucolics* refers without doubt to this precise moment.
The poem purports to be, above all, a thank-offer-
ing of the Poet to Octavian for the recovery of his
confiscated lands; it also conveys to the powerful
triumvir, with an infinite tact and no suspicion of

---

[1] Servius Danielis, on *Ecl.* IX, 7: "Usque ad eum locum per-
ticam limitarem Octavius Musa porrexerat, limitator ab Augusto datus, id est per quindecim milia passuum agri Mantuani,
cum Cremonensis non sufficeret."

[2] I think that we may thus dispose not only of the contradiction between *manebunt* (*Ecl.* I, 46) and *servasse* (*Ecl.* IX, 10),
noted by modern interpreters, but also of the theory of the
restitution to which the ancient biographers and commentators
constantly refer. See below, Appendix II.

[3] On *Ecl.* IX, 10: "OMNIA, quae supra dixit. Intelligamus
autem aut Vergilii tantum agrum, aut totius Mantuae descrip-
tum. . . . OMNIA CARMINIBUS VESTRUM SERVASSE MENALCAM,
id est vestrum Vergilium, *cuius causa agri Mantuanis redditi
sunt.*"

ingratitude, the plaint of his oppressed country.

The *Tityrus* is true and spontaneous poetry; Theocritean phrasing, which recurs now and then, is no longer studied imitation, but simple and unconscious reminiscence due to the Poet's familiarity with his master. In the background is Mantuan landscape, faintly touched with Alexandrine color. Mantuan are the two speakers and all their discourses refer to Mantua. We have no longer a simple lyric drama made up of pastoral songs, as in most of the preceding eclogues. The drama of *Tityrus* is touched with tragic feeling which the hymn to the Roman god does not disguise.

The plot of the poem is depicted in the very first verses by the contrast presented. The fortunate shepherd who reposes in the shade of a beech and sets woodland songs to the slender pipe is contrasted with the unhappy exile, who, driven from the pleasant fields, is constrained to flee his country. A god has granted this peace to Tityrus; thanks to that god his cattle can graze tranquilly and he can pipe at will on his rustic flute. But round about him all is confusion in the fields; and the shepherds, expelled from their lands, drive before them on the road to their exile the few goats that they were able to snatch from the rapacious invaders.

How could the lucky shepherd escape the common plight? With profound reverence, almost with trepidation, the humble herdsman of Mantua pronounces a glorious name: Rome. Rome lifts her brow above the other cities, as any cypress above the bending viburnum: from Rome the shepherd received his freedom; in Rome he sees the young god who to his prayer makes the gracious response: pasture your oxen as of old, my lads, rear your bulls.

Fortunate shepherd, indeed; to him will remain his fields, ample enough for him, although all the pastures be covered with bare gravel or muddy rush of the fen. But we, sighs the fugitive, shall go wandering about in distant countries, amongst inhospitable peoples; and who knows if, after long years, I shall see again the roof of my poor hut heaped with turf, and in the fields which were all my realm I shall find only a few spikes of corn? These fallow fields, cultivated with such care and such love, shall they fall into the hands of some rough soldier, who will make havoc with them? Shall a barbarian enjoy these harvests? Lo, to what a wretched pass has civil discord brought us! Lo, for whose profit have we sown our fields! Engraft thy pear-trees, O Meliboeus, set thy vines in row! The detachment of the peasant from his land could not be more sympathetically described. The fugitive abandons his fields with the anguish of one who leaves a beloved person, for whom he fears almost more than for himself. And after the lament for

the fields, he turns to the flocks who will stay there,
deprived of their shepherd:

> Move on, dear flock, whose happy days are done!
> My mother-goats, move on!   No more shall I
> Reclined in cool, green cave behold from far
> How on the bush-grown crag you cling and climb.
> No shepherd-songs for me!   I shall not lead
> My feeding mother-goats to get their fill
> Of clover-buds or willow's bitter stem.

The Tityrus of this beautiful poem, although a
pastoral character, surely represents in some traits
the Poet himself. But the allegory, very transpar-
ent when there is any, should not be as Servius
wisely warns us, extended to the whole eclogue;[1]
this admonition did not receive the attention it
merited by the ancient scholiasts, to whom, truth
to tell, Servius himself set not a few examples of
extravagance in his search for the allegorical sense
in this as in the other eclogues.

When Virgil wrote *Tityrus*, he had fondly hoped
that his land was not to be taken from him. But
he was soon to learn to his own cost, that poetry,
to which he attributed his salvation, had but small
effect on the minds of the rough soldiers who had
taken possession of his lands. And what could Octavian do from Rome? What could the Triumvirs

---

[1] On line 1: "Et hoc loco Tityri sub persona Vergilium debe-
mus accipere; non tamen ubique, sed tantum ubi exigit ratio."
On the extravagances of the ancient commentators in their
hunt for the supposed allegorical allusions in this poem, see
Funaioli, *Allegorie Virgiliane*, pp. 159–164.

in charge of the confiscated lands avail against the
greedy and powerful veterans? We do not know
whether, after his return from Rome, Virgil found
it possible to recover possession of his little farm,
or what were the new disputes which had arisen
amongst the veterans. The *Ninth Eclogue* tells us
that Menalcas, who this time impersonates Virgil
throughout the poem, had preserved all his property[1]— so ran the report.

The phrase *audieras et fama fuit* would seem to
attest the contrary. According to Servius,[2] and
apparently Donatus,[3] these new disputes coincided
with the moment when Virgil had just returned
from Rome. Fortified by the concession from Augustus, and supported by his faithful steward, he
attempted to reoccupy his property, only to find
that in the meantime it had been seized by the cen-

[1] *Ecl.* IX, 7–10.

[2] *Prooem. in Bucol.* "Perdito ergo agro Vergilius Romam
venit et potentium favore meruit, ut agrum suum solus reciperet, ad quem accipiendum profectus, ab Arrio centurione, qui
eum tenebat, paene est interemptus, nisi se praecipitasset in
Mincium. . . . Postea ab Augusto missis tribus viris et ipsi
integer ager est redditus et Mantuanis pro parte."

[3] Brummer, pp. 15–16: "Vergilius merito carminum fretus et
amicitia quorundam potentium centurioni Arrio cum obsistere
ausus esset ille statim, ut miles, ad gladium manum admovit,
cumque se in fugam proripuisset poeta, non prius finis perse-
quendi fuit, quam se in fluvium Vergilius coniecisset, atque ita
in alteram ripam enatavisset. Sed postea per Maecenatem et
per triumviros agris dividendis Varum, Pollionem et Cornelium Gallum fama carminum commendatus Augusto et agros
recepit et deinceps imperatoris familiari amore perfruitus est."

turion Arrius, or some other in his stead. In the conflict that ensued, the centurion unsheathed his sword and proceeded to chase out the ingenuous Poet, who was forced to save himself by plunging into the Mincio.[1] Whatever the truth of this last episode, it is certain, from the words of Virgil himself, that both he and his steward were in danger of being killed had they not cut short the dispute in time.[2]

The *Ninth Eclogue, Moeris*, to those who read it without being influenced by ancient or modern commentators, appears a sequel to the first, to which it evidently refers in verses seven and eleven. It is a dialogue between two shepherds on their way to the city, which can be none other than Mantua. One, Moeris, steward of Virgil, is carrying on his shoulders a pair of kids for the new master; the other, Lycidas, is a young shepherd of the neighborhood, also on his way to town. The conversation takes place on the road that leads into Mantua. The first beat of the song could not be better contrived:

Where bound, my Moeris? Runs thy road to town?

To the demand of his friend, the steward of Menalcas replies with a sigh:

[1] On the variants of this episode in the ancient commentators, see Appendix II.
[2] *Ecl.* IX, 14–16.

O Lycidas, today we live to see
Something we never feared — a foreigner
Holding our little farm, who harshly cries,
"These lands are mine. Ye dwellers of old time,
Away with you!" And we submit to this,
We wretched ones; for Chance and Fortune's power
Change all things.   We are sending him today
Two kids — and may the gift no blessing be!

There was a rumor, it is true, that Menalcas, as
a recompense for his songs, had rescued his property from the point where the hills begin to retire
and lower their ridge in a soft slope, even to the
waterside and the old beeches with their broken
crests. Thus went the rumor, yes, but the master
and his steward just missed losing their lives.

Lycidas is deeply moved by the risk run by Menalcas. What a loss to poetry if Menalcas had been
slain! Who, had he died, would sing the Nymphs or
the earth strewn with grass and flowers, or shaded
springs? At the moment, the shepherd-poet who
gladdened the life of the fields with his song, is far
away; but the two fellow-travellers recall some
themes of his poetry. With this cunning device,
Virgil can remind Varus discreetly, almost without
appearing to, of the vain hope placed in him for the
salvation of Mantua; and he makes Octavian consider that very little benefit had come to the Poet
for being a friend of Caesar's:

Daphni, quid antiquos signorum suspicis ortus?
Ecce Dionaei processit Caesaris astrum,

astrum, quo segetes gauderent frugibus et quo
duceret apricis in collibus uva colorem.
Insere, Daphni, piros: carpent tua poma nepotes.

What bitterness is hidden in the last verse just sung
by the servant of Menalcas! Engraft thy pear-
trees, O Daphnis; thy grand-children shall gather
the fruits! How can we help but recall the bitter
words of Meliboeus in the *First Eclogue:*

Insere nunc, Meliboee, piros, pone ordine vites!

The memory of the songs of Menalcas, arouses
in Lycidas the desire to sing. He too makes verses
and the shepherds proclaim him a poet. All the
plain is silent and round about every slight mur-
mur of the breeze has died away. They are halfway
to the city when already they begin to see the tomb
of Bianor. Why not rest a little and refresh themselves with song, in the shade of the hedge, there
where the peasants are pruning the dense branches?
And if, then, it befits them to continue their way,
song will make the road all the sweeter. But the
heart of Moeris is too sad to accept the invitation:

Carmina tum melius, cum venerit ipse, canemus.

The plot of *Moeris* is taken from the *Seventh
Idyll* of Theocritus, in which Simichidas, on the
way to the house of friends to celebrate Demeter's
feast, Thalysia, meets Lycidas. Continuing their
journey together they exchange songs of their own
invention; then they separate, taking different

roads, Simichidas going to his friends' house. Some
details are also imitated from the same idyll.[1] The
substance of the poem, however, is profoundly original. The drama, unfolding itself in a Theocritean
setting, is intimately connected with the life of the
Poet; the sentiments that inspired the two poems
are as different as the situation of their characters,
Moeris and Simichidas. One might almost say that
the imitation is for once pure artifice, studiously
designed to temper the stern reality.

Where was Virgil when he wrote this poem? Certainly not at Mantua, as he himself implies. The
brutal order *"veteres migrate coloni"* given by the
veteran who occupied his property, had forced him,
like Meliboeus, to a life of exile. The poem in the
Catalepton above mentioned,[2] which, even if it was
not written by Virgil, contains ancient evidence of
high value, represents the Poet at Rome with his
dear ones and his old father, seeking a tranquil
refuge after the storm. In the little villa which once
was Siro's, he can place his family in security,
while he waits for better news from Mantua.

Villula, quae Sironis eras, et pauper agelle,
    verum illi domino tu quoque divitiae,
me tibi et hos una mecum, quos semper amavi,
    si quid de patria tristius audiero,
commendo, in primisque patrem. Tu nunc eris illi
    Mantua quod fuerat quodque Cremona prius.

---

[1] Cf. Cartault, pp. 376 ff.
[2] See above, pp. 14 and 36.

With regard to Virgil's family, the ancient biographers and the scholiasts inform us that the Poet had at least three brothers, Silo, Flaccus, and Valerius Proculus, this latter a half-brother on his mother's side. As for his parents, we know that they died when Virgil was no longer a youth, and that the father had become blind.[1] It is not impossible then that both parents might have been alive when the spoliation occurred. Of Silo, it is said that he died when a very young boy, that Flaccus was somewhat older at his death, and that Virgil mourns his death in the *Fifth Eclogue*.[2] This interpretation of the eclogue may be, as is generally believed, a simple conjecture of the commentators, which for all that would not interfere with the truth of the previous assertion. To his half-brother, Valerius Proculus, he left at his death the half of his patrimony. It should be added that the existence of this half-brother, whom Probus considers younger than Virgil, has raised problems for modern scholars, problems which arise, in the main, from the desire to reconcile the statements of the ancient biogra-

[1] Brummer, pp. 3, 44 ff.: "Parentes iam grandis amisit, ex quibus patrem captum oculis, et duos fratres germanos, Silonem impuberem, Flaccum iam adultum, cuius exitum sub nomine Daphnidis deflet." According to Philargyrius, quoted by the *Scholia Bernensia* on *Ecl.* V, 22, the mother must have died shortly after Flaccus: "Superstite enim Maia matre Flaccus defunctus est, quae eius mortem graviter ferens non diu supervixit. Iunilius dicit."

[2] Cf. the *Scholia Bernensia*, Servius and Philargyrius on *Ecl.* V, 1, 20. See the preceding note.

phers and scholiasts with the passage in the *Catalepton* referred to above.[1]

When Virgil wrote the *Ninth Eclogue*, he doubtless hoped to regain the possession of his property;
this alone can be the meaning of the last words of
Moeris: *Cum venerit ipse.* But, were his fields restored to him? Probus, Donatus, and Servius, together with the ancient scholiasts, assert that they
were;[2] but their testimony leaves much uncertainty, for two reasons. First, it seems to be based
chiefly on the *First Eclogue*, and not to take suffi-
cient account of the *Ninth*, wherein we are assured
that Virgil's hope of retaining his property was
frustrated. The second reason is that Virgil does
not give in his later works the slightest hint of the
restoration supposed to have occurred after *Moeris*.
On the contrary, when, in the second book of the
Georgics, he mentions the pastures fit for flocks and
herds, including the meadows of Tarentum, the
memory comes to him — and the memory is tinged

[1] Cf. Cartault, pp. 7 ff.; Diehl, p. 13.

[2] Donatus (Brummer, p. 5): "Quia in distributione agrorum
. . . indemnem se praestitissent [i.e. Asinius Pollio, Alfenus
Varus, and Cornelius Gallus]." *Ibid.*, p. 16: "Postea et per
Maecenatem et per triumviros agris dividendis Varum, Pollionem et Cornelium Gallum . . . agros recepit." Servius, *Vita*
(*Ibid.*, p. 69): "Amissis ergo agris, Romam venit et . . . solus
agrum quem amiserat meruit" (see above, p. 92). Probus,
Praef. ad Bucol. (Thilo and Hagen, III, 2, 328): "Promeruit ut
agros suos reciperet"; *Vita* (Brummer, p. 73): "Postea resti-
tutus." We should note that Probus considers the *Ninth
Eclogue* as written before the *First;* this opinion is shared among
the moderns by Nettleship, Krause, and Duchâtaux.

with regret — of the fields that Mantua lost, fields
that fed the snowy swans along the grassy river
banks.[1] Any direct allusion to the place of his birth,
which contained a wealth of subjects for poetry, is
entirely lacking in the matter of the *Georgics*, as
though the thought of his birthplace were painful.
To Mantua he promised to return some day,
crowned with laurels; but in his very words — *in
patriam . . . modo vita supersit . . . rediens* — his
hope is expressed with a sigh.[2]

It is certain, at all events, that from that moment
we meet Virgil no more in Mantua, unless it be in
memory and desire. Donatus informs us that the
Poet, although he had a house in Rome on the Es-
quiline near the park of Maecenas, spent the greater
part of his time in the villas which he had in Cam-
pania and in Sicily.[3] Although the wealth of Virgil,
born poor, is attributed by the biographers to the
liberality of his friends, especially of Octavian and
of Maecenas,[4] it is probable that after the facts to

---

[1] *Georg.*, II, 198–199:
  "Et qualem infelix amisit Mantua campum
  pascentem niveos herboso flumine cycnos."

[2] See above, p. 16.

[3] Brummer, p. 3: "Possedit prope centies sestertium ex lib-
eralitate amicorum habuitque domum Romae Esquiliis iuxta
hortos Maecenationas, quamquam secessu Campaniae Sici-
liaeque plurimum uteretur." Aulus Gellius (VI, 20) assures us
that the Poet had a villa at Nola.

[4] See the preceding note, and Martial VIII, 55 (56), 7:
  "Iugera perdiderat miserae vicina Cremonae,
  flebat et abductas Tityrus aeger oves:

which the *Ninth Eclogue* alludes, they thought to
indemnify him for the loss of his fields by offering
him other lands in Southern Italy, without provok-
ing new and dangerous conflicts with the veterans.
And perhaps it is to this moment that Donatus refers when he says that Virgil had not the heart to
accept the goods of an exile that Octavian offered
him.[1]

> Risit Tuscus eques, paupertatemque malignam
> reppulit et celeri iussit abire fuga.
> 'Accipe divitias et vatum maximus esto'."

[1] Brummer, p. 3, l. 39: "Bona autem cuiusdam exulantis
offerente Augusto non sustinuit accipere."

IV. Ite, Capellae

SUMMARY: 1. The last labor: *Gallus.* — 2. Maecenas. Virgil amongst his new friends. His portrait, physical and moral.

1

WITH the *Ninth Eclogue*, written probably toward the end of 39, or at the latest at the beginning of 38 B.C., the series of pastoral poems would seem to be complete; and if one was lacking, it was that which awaited the return of Menalcas:

Carmina tum melius, cum venerit ipse, canemus.

But this song was never composed and the reason for it is clear: Menalcas never returned to occupy his little farm amongst his faithful servants.

When the Poet had been compensated for the loss of his property and finding leisure once more began to sing again, his song is a farewell to the pastoral muse; the poem, partly bucolic and partly elegiac, is inspired by his friendship for Gallus. The *Tenth Eclogue* seems to have been written in 37 B.C. since it was not before the beginning of that year that Lycoris abandoned Gallus to follow a rough soldier, enduring the Alpine snows and the rigors of the

101

Rhine.[1] For that was the time that Agrippa, sent
into Gaul as a legate of Octavian, crossed the
Rhone, the first of the Roman generals who dared
that feat after Caesar. His purpose was to protect
the Ubii, whom the dangerous Suebi continuously
harassed. Thus the *Gallus* would seem to fall outside the three years assigned to the composition of
the *Bucolics*.[2] This result, however, does not repudi-
ate the united testimony of the ancient grammarians, if we interpret that testimony with discretion.
It seems to me that a pause of silence may have
intervened between the *Ninth Eclogue* and the *Gallus*, as is indicated by the "*concede*" of the first
verse, addressed to the nymph Arethusa. The Poet
seeks her favor for a "last labor," after he had
thought his pastorals were done.

The praises of Gallus as a poet were sung by Silenus in the admirable *Sixth Eclogue*, dedicated to
Alfenus Varus. The last poem is a song of friendship, devoted and sweet, between two souls trans-
parent to each other, that drew closer together the
greater their need. I do not think that Cornelius
Gallus had said to Virgil: "I am in despair, make
me some verses." I believe instead that the Mantuan, when he understood the pain of his friend,
had divined that he must soothe it with song.

[1] Lines 22–23: "Tua cura Lycoris | perque nives alium perque
horrida castra secuta est." Lines 47–48: "Alpinas, ah, dura
nives et frigora Rheni | me sine sola vides."
[2] See above, p. 49.

Soothe it? Modern critics ask what Virgil meant
to do in the *Gallus*. One scholar has discovered
there a parody of the very realistic love that Gallus had for the dancer, Cytheris; his passion placed
in the pastoral setting of Theocritus, should make
the friend of Virgil laugh, and find in laughter the
healing for his ills. However, this interpretation of
the eclogue ill agrees either with the serious and
affectionate tone of the introduction and of the
conclusion, or with the note of sincere compassion
for the pain of Gallus which breathes throughout
the poem. Shall we say, then, that the *Tenth Eclogue* is written for the purpose of detaching Gallus
from his mad love by showing him the vanity of it?
It would not seem so, since Gallus is exalted in his
passion and at the end of the poem not only remains
enamored and unhappy as before, but proclaims as
a veritable law of fate:

> Omnia vincit amor et nos cedamus amori!

Virgil's poem is neither an inappropriate parody,
nor is it, properly speaking, a poem of consolation.[1]
It is a delicate expression of the Poet's profound
comprehension of the torment which comes to Gallus through disappointed love for a woman, whom,
although unworthy of him, he loved with intense
affection and of whom he had sung in sweet elegies.
In this eclogue, too, Gallus is an elegiac poet, and

[1] Cf. Cartault, pp. 383 ff.

such he remains. Virgil shows an understanding of
the friend and the poet in this his last bucolic song,
which flows from his pure heart; his love for Gallus
grows from hour to hour, even as the green alders
in springtime.

In the *Gallus*, Virgil for the first time unmistak-
ably pictures himself as a shepherd. He sits there
weaving a little basket from pliant rushes, while
the flat-nosed goats crop the tender bushes; the
forest repeats the song. At the rising of the star of
Vesper, the shepherd ceases his song and leads
back the goats to the fold:

Ite domum saturae, venit Hesperus, ite, capellae.

2

Ite, capellae. It is not improbable that in these
words, placed, as they are, at the end of the last
bucolic poem, we have, besides their literal meaning, the sense of a farewell to pastoral poetry and
the muse of Theocritus. Pollio had incited the
young poet to compete with the Syracusan. Obe-
dient to this suggestion of his friend and protector,
Virgil had enriched Roman literature with a new
kind of poetry, in which he had given ample proof
of his power. Nor had he been a servile imitator of
Theocritus. To have contaminated, as the grammarians say, pastoral poetry with elements extran-
neous to it, even with political and military events,

is his greatest merit; for these contaminations revealed in him the capacity and the desire to risk an arduous emprise. A simple imitation of Theocritus in Rome, in the midst of events like those to which we have alluded, would have been a frivolous rhetorical exercise, not of poetry. Virgil himself realized the boldness of his youthful attempt.[1]

As soon as they were known, the *Eclogues* met with great success. Donatus informs us[2] that they were often declaimed on the stage, and Tacitus adds that once when the spectators in the theatre heard the verses of Virgil, they rose to their feet, and since the Poet was present, they acclaimed him as if he had been Augustus.[3]

When he fled from Mantua, Virgil had in Maecenas a new friend and protector. Scion of the ancient Etruscan race, a mild and noble spirit, devoted to the reposeful studies and endowed with practical sense, he held the two keys to Caesar's heart. The choice souls who lived then in Rome found a cordial reception and munificent hospitality in his palace. The Poet, thanks to him, if he could not recover his

---

[1] *Georg.*, IV, 565–566:
  "Carmina qui lusi pastorum audaxque inventa,
    Tityre, te patulae cecini sub tegmine fagi."
[2] Brummer, p. 6, l. 90: "Bucolica eo successu edidit, ut in scaena quoque per cantores crebro pronuntiarentur."
[3] Tacitus, *Dial. de orator.*, XIII: "Testis ipse populus, qui auditis in theatro Vergilii versibus surrexit universus et forte praesentem spectantemque Vergilium veneratus est sic quasi Augustum."

paternal possessions, obtained at least so large a
recompense that he was enabled to dedicate himself to poetry with peace of mind. From Maecenas, likewise, he received the impulse to undertake
a work of a substance quite different from that of
the pastoral poems — to apply the divine music of
his verse to singing the wearing toils that stir the
earth to fecundity.

Among those who frequented the literary sym-
posium of this friend and adviser of Octavian, were
Horace, Varius, Rufus, Plotius Tucca, and Quintilius Varus. They became the most devoted friends
of Virgil, and from now on we see him in their company.[1] They all were worthy of him. The pleasant
journey from Rome to Brundisium, described for
us by Horace, took place probably in 37 B.C.[2] At
Anxur the Poet is joined by Maecenas together
with Cocceius and Fronteius; they take to the road
again and on the fourth day, at Sinuessa, they meet
Plotius, Varius, and Virgil, the purest souls, exclaims Horace, that have ever appeared on the
earth.[3] The party of friends lodged at night in a
little villa near the Campanian bridge on the Ap-

---

[1] Probus, *Vita* (Brummer, p. 73): "Insigni concordia et fa-
miliaritate usus Quintili, Tuccae et Vari."

[2] *Saturnalia*, 1, 5.

[3] Lines 39–42:

"Postera lux oritur multo gratissima; namque
Plotius et Varius Sinuessae Vergiliusque
occurrunt animae quales neque candidiores
terra tulit neque quis me sit devinctior alter."

pian Way. While Maecenas goes to play, Horace
and Virgil go to bed; for a game of ball, Horace
jokingly remarks, is injurious to the blear-eyed,
like himself, and to those who have weak stomachs,
like Virgil.[1]

This allusion to the delicate health of Virgil
tallies with the statements of Donatus. The latter
sketches for us a physical and moral portrait of our
Poet, which, if not exact in everything, has at least,
in all probability, preserved some of the original
traits.

The physical appearance of Virgil has been
sketched by Donatus with a few light touches: the
Poet was tall of stature and sturdy of limb, brown
of color, with the look of a peasant.[2] If Donatus
really depends here on Suetonius, it is probable
that these traits correspond to the truth, since at
the time of the author of the *Lives of the Caesars*
there was no lack of portraits and statues of the
Poet.[3] Nor should we disguise the fact that the portrait preserved in the mosaic of Hadrumetum,[4]
corresponds very well with that traced by Donatus.
The biographer adds still another characteristic:
his delicate health — the Poet often suffered with

[1] *Ibid.*, vv. 45–49.

[2] Brummer, p. 2: "Corpore et statura fuit grandi, aquilo
colore, facie rusticana."

[3] Cf. Martial XIV, 186; Suetonius, *Calig.*, 34, 2; Lampridius,
Alex. Sev., 31, 4.

[4] Schulten, *Arch. Anz.* (1899), 70. See also the article of
C. Pascal in *Lettura*, XXVI, 11 (Nov. 1, 1926), pp. 835 ff.

his stomach, with his throat, and with headache, and often coughed up blood.[1] We have also noted the sweetness of his voice in declaiming.[2]

As to the moral portrait, I think we must make allowances for what Donatus and the scholastics say, especially as regards the Poet's pretended penchant for boys.[3] Except for this fault, Servius tells us, his life was blameless.[4] Donatus affirms that he was very moderate in his food and drink. The episode, taken from Asconius Pedianus, of the rejection by Virgil of the advances made to him by Plotia Hieria or Leria, is not very clear;[5] and the charge of his addiction to the *libido in pueros*, makes us suspect that Donatus has misrepresented the sense of the episode, if it be true. The same biographer, after echoing the salacious remarks that were current in the schools of the grammarians, ventures to add that, for the rest, our Poet was so modest in his manner and in his feeling, that in

[1] Brummer, p. 3: "Valetudine varia; nam plerumque a stomacho et a faucibus et dolore capitis laborabat; sanguinem etiam saepe reiecit."

[2] Brummer, pp. 6–7: "Pronountiabat autem cum suavitate, cum lenociniis miris; ac Seneca tradidit Iulium Montanum poetam solitum dicere, involaturum se Vergilio quaedam si et vocem posset et os et hypocrisin."

[3] Cf. above, pp. 62 f.

[4] Brummer, p. 68: "Omni vita probatus, uno tantum morbo laborabat; nam inpatiens libidinis fuit."

[5] Brummer, p. 3: "Vulgatum est consuesse eum et cum Plotia Hieria; sed Asconius Pedianus adfirmat, ipsam postea maiorem natu narrare solitam, invitatum quidem a Vario ad communionem sui, verum pertinacissime recusasse."

Naples they were wont to call him commonly by a Greek name, Parthenias, the virgin. He adds that when he went to Rome — a thing that happened rarely — and his admirers made a demonstration in his honor and followed him about, he would escape into the nearest house.[1] Nor must we forget the other trait of his moral physiognomy which well agrees with his rusticity of appearance — he was embarrassed in speaking, just like a rough country lad.[2]

For all that, this timid and pensive rustic whom Mantua sent to Rome, in recompense for the unjust spoliations, conquered his natural reticence when he was with a few chosen friends, and gave vent to the flood of music which surged in his breast, arousing admiration by the suavity of his song. If Alexander wept at the tomb of Achilles, because he had lacked his Homer, the son of the divine Caesar could call himself much more fortunate,—for he had found in Virgil a singer who could exalt to the stars his name and that of Rome.

[1] Brummer, p. 3: "Cetera sane vitae et ore et animo tam probum, ut Neapoli Parthenias vulgo appellatus sit, ac si quando Romae, quo rarissime commeabat, viseretur in publico, sectantis demonstrantisque se suffugeret in proximum tectum."

[2] See above, p. 35, n. 1.

APPENDICES

APPENDIX I

VIRGIL'S BIRTHPLACE

1. *The Earliest Mention of Andes*

THE earliest statement about Virgil's birthplace is, without doubt, that contained in the *Life* of the Poet prefixed as an introduction to the comment of Valerius Probus on the *Bucolics.* The authenticity and the historical value of this *Life* have been warmly debated; the names of Riese,[1] Norden,[2] Ribbeck,[3] Thilo,[4] Aisterman,[5] will suggest the diverse views that have been entertained. It is generally agreed, nevertheless, that except for some evident interpolations the substance of the life is authentic.[6] This admission attributes a high value to the *Life*, when we remember that Valerius Probus, of Berytus, lived in the time of Nero and of the Flavians, and that his commentary must have been known to the other early biographers and commentators of Virgil.

[1] *De commentario Verg. qui M. V. Probi dicitur dissert.*(Bonn, 1862).

[2] *Rhein. Mus.*, LXI (1906), 171.

[3] *Fleckeis. Jahrb.*, LXXXVII (1863), 351. See also his *Prolegomena critica ad P. Verg. Mar. opera maiora* (Lipsiae, 1866), pp. 163–164.

[4] *Fleckeis. Jahrb.*, CXLIX (1894), 290 ff.

[5] *De M. V. Probi vita et scriptis* (Bonn, 1909), pp. 70 ff.

[6] Cf. Aistermann, *loc. cit.*

One reason why Norden denied the authenticity
of the life of Virgil attributed to Probus, is that we
find there the statement that the Mantuan Poet
was born in the *"vico Andico qui abest a Mantua,
milia passuum XXX."* Evidently, as Norden
thought, such a blunder cannot be attributed to
Probus, who, as Suetonius assures us, was a most
diligent investigator and possessed a copy of Virgil's poetry corrected by the author himself. If
Andes were found to be thirty Roman miles from
Mantua, Virgil would certainly have been born
outside the province of Mantua; he would then
have hardly been called a Mantuan, as he himself
professes to be, but rather a native of Verona, or
Brescia, or Cremona, or Modena.[1] Besides, the
"milia passuum XXX"— a not inconsiderable distance — runs counter to the united testimony of
the other ancient biographers. Thus in the life
written by Donatus, taken largely from the one by
Suetonius which is lost, we read that Andes was
not far from Mantua,[2] and precisely the same state-

---

[1] It might be said, and one scholar has said it, that Virgil was
called Mantuan, not because he was born at Mantua, but because his parents lived there, or because he finally established
himself there. However, the ancient biographers considered
him a Mantuan because he was born in the village of Andes,
near to Mantua. Thus they understand the words *"Mantua me
genuit"* of the noted distich incised on his tomb, which, according to Donatus, must have been written by the Poet himself.
See above, pp. 15 f.

[2] Brummer, p. 1: "A Mantua non procul."

ment is repeated by St. Jerome.[1] The "not far" of
Donatus and St. Jerome becomes explicitly a
"prope" in a manuscript of the ninth century[2] and
a *"iuxta"* in one of the tenth.[3]

To put thirty Roman miles, then, between Andes
and Mantua is an error, or even, as Diehl thinks,
an absurdity.[4] However, this error might easily
have been eliminated if the modern German philol-
ogists who created the problem had been a trifle
more thorough. Hagen, for his critical edition of
the commentary of Probus on Virgil, used three
manuscripts of the fifteenth century and one of
these, the Munich codex, is of the year 1496–97; all
these sources, therefore, are recent. Hagen also
makes use of the edition of Egnatius published in
Venice in 1507.[5] Now this edition is of great value,
because it is based on an ancient codex, found at

[1] Hier., *Chron., Olymp.* CLXXVII, 4 (Schoene, II, 155):
"Haud procul a Mantua."

[2] *Vita Gudiana* III (Brummer, p. 64): "in oppido prope
Mantua[m]."

[3] *Vita Monacensis*, Brummer, p. 56: "In pago Andensi in
villa quae Andis dicitur iuxta Mantuam."

[4] E. Diehl, *Die Vitae Vergilianae*, p. 9: "ein nonsens."

[5] An edition earlier than that of Egnatius was published in
Rome, in 1471 (cf. *P. Vergili Maronis Opera, ex recens.* Chr. G.
Heyne *recentioribus Wunderlinchii et Ruhkopfii curis illustrata*
[Turin: Pomba, 1827], vol. I, pp. cxxxi f.). This rare incuna-
bulum, possessed by the Laurentian Library in Florence, was
collated for me by Professor Flaminio Pellegrini, to whom I ex-
press thanks. This edition, too, has *"milia passuum XXX."*
From an examination of the variants, I am inclined to believe
that this edition comes from the Vatican manuscript, of the
fifteenth century, or from some other closely connected with it.

Bobbio by the humanist Georgio Merula, which
from certain features of the Venice edition seems
to have been a veritable treasure even in its imper-
fection.[1] Now Hagen, who includes in his apparatus the readings of the aforesaid manuscripts and
the Venice edition, passes by in silence the most
important variant from the last-named source, on
just the point that concerns us. For the Venice edi-

---

[1] P. V. M. *Bucolica, Georgica, Aeneis cum Servii commentariis
accuratissime emendatis, in quibus multa, quae deerant, sunt ad-
dita. Graecae dictiones et versus ubique restituti. Seq. Probi, cele-
bris grammatici, in Bucolica et Georgica commentariolus non antea
impressus*, etc. Venetiis, Io. Bapt. Egnatius Venetus emendavit.
Colophon: *Venetiis excusi M. D. VII, die ultimo Iunii. Bernar-
dinus Stagninus impensam fecit.* In the preface *ad lectorem*, Egnatius informs us that in reproducing the commentary of Probus he has respected the *vetustas* of the codex of Bobbio: "In
bucolicis, quod ad Probi commentariolum attinet, secuti sumus
vetustatem illam quemadmodum ex *vetustissimo* codice manu
scripto Bobii, quondam a Georgio Merula invento, *adnotavi-
mus.*" That he did so really for all that concerns the life of
Virgil is made evident not only by a fine *quoius* left in the place
of the *cujus*, which is read in all manuscripts known today and
in the Roman edition of 1471, but also by his having left blank
two spaces corresponding to two evident lacunae, or more probably to words become unintelligible, in the ancient codex of
Bobbio. The edition of Egnatius was reproduced many times
in the course of the sixteenth century. Probus' life of Virgil is
also found in an edition of the early years of the seventeenth
century, published at Cologne (*P. Virgilii Maronis Opera
omnia*, Coloniae apud Gosuinum Cholinum anno MDCIII),
with the title *P. Virgilii Maronis ex Probo grammatico fragmen-
tum.* This edition also has "*milia passuum tria.*" From a comparison with the edition of Egnatius, I am induced to believe
that this is the source on which the Cologne edition depends;
the editor has also attempted to fill in the more important
lacuna, just as Keil and Thilo did later.

tion, on the strength of the old Bobbio manuscript, reads that Andes is distant from Mantua *"milia passuum iij,"* that is to say, three Roman miles.[1] In other words, the evidence of the manuscripts, when rightly understood, supports the popular tradition.

2. *Ancient Virgilian Traditions about Pietole*

The popular tradition which places in the village of Pietole, near the banks of the Mincio, the house and the farm where Virgil was born did not originate, as many hold, in the time of Dante, but has its roots in statements — whether true or not matters little — transmitted by the early biographers and commentators. This tradition, represented by various local legends, testifies to an ancient cult of the Poet maintained by the inhabitants of the village. The evidence for such a tradition is submitted herewith to the reader.

According to Donatus and Focas, some held that

[1] In what manner a III or a tr^a could have become a XXX is not difficult to explain palaeographically: further, one need not mention the fate that, in the diverse mediaeval manuscripts and redactions of the *Life* by Donatus, befell the numbers that indicated the age in which the youthful works were written. Cf. Brummer, p. 4. This same distance, *"III milliaria,"* was officially fixed in the Middle Ages between Mantua (quarter of San Martino) and Pietole. Cf. *Statuta Dominorum Raynaldi et Botironi Fratrum de Bonacolsis*, Lib. VII, rubr. 52, De milliariis villarum, De quarterio Sancti Martini, in C. D'Arco, *Storia di Mantova*, III; 204.

the father of Virgil was a *figulus*,[1] a potter. Now
this statement might have some connection with
the ancient name of *Fornicatula* (changed to *Fornicata* and then *Formicata* and *Formigada*) given to a
very large farm near Pietole described in a document of the eleventh century studied by Carreri.[2]
It is very probable that such a name might be the
diminutive of *fornax*, "oven" "kiln." It is well
known not only that the district of Pietole and
Formigada is a land of kilns, but also that the memory of not a few old kilns survives there; further,
the existence of abundant ancient potteries has
been shown by Carreri.[3] Therefore, the statement

[1] See above, p. 8.

[2] F. Carreri, *Pietole*, etc. (See "List of Works Frequently
Cited," p. xi), pp. 24 ff. *Ibid.*, p. 43 (a document of 1231):
"Prata seu loca sive Pletularum sive Fornicate." *Ibid.*, p. 44
(a document of 1238): "in territorio pretularum apud Fornica-
tulas." *Ibid.*, p. 46 (a document of 1217): "homines Pletularum
et Furnicate." See also Carreri's article, *De luco Virgilii in
agro pletulensi sacrando* (extract from *Classici e Neolatini*, VI
[1910], 2–3), Aosta, 1910, pp. 4 ff.

[3] Carreri, *Pietole, Formigada*, etc., p. 27; *De luco*, p. 6. The
etymology is not certain. Carreri suggests another in the bar-
barous word *fornakar*, which signifies less-cultivated districts.
Dal Zotto holds that *Fornicata* is derived from *fornix*, used by
Frontinus (*De Aquaeductu Urbis Romae*) to signify air hydraulic
work (*R. Accademia Virgiliana di Mantova, Atti e Memorie*,
N. S., XIX-XX, 246). *Fornicata* might thus be the past partici-
ple of the verb *fornicare* in the sense of *fornices extruere*. Perhaps the ditch mentioned in the mediaeval documents was, for
part of its extent, covered with an archway, or, to use an expression of Sallust's, *lapideis fornicibus iuncta*. But whatever
may be thought of these etymologies, it seems none the less
likely that the statement of the ancient biographers with re-

of ancient biographers that Virgil's father was a potter may have some connection with the prevalence of the art of pottery among the inhabitants of Andes.

The document studied by Carreri contains a bit of topographical evidence important for its bearing on the popular tradition. It concerns the confines of the farm called Fornicata: "Ipsa namque curte suam habet diffinitionem per fossatum quod vocatur fornicatula, quod percurrit usque ad fossatum quod vocatur Virgilii, a fossato Virgilii usque ad casaleclo."[1]

After much pondering of this important document, I began to wonder whether the Virgil from whom the ditch takes its name might be some landed proprietor of the place rather than the Poet. But after having turned over not a few mediaeval records, I perceived to my great surprise that among the several thousand names of persons, especially those of witnesses, no *Virgilius* of any sort or description ever once appears. One might guess that

gard to the occupation of Virgil's father was based on the fact that in antiquity as today there were ovens at Andes. In corroboration of Carreri's arguments it may be added that a certain Boninsegna de Cita, *fornexarius*, is mentioned as a potter (*fittavolo*) at Pietole in a document of the middle of the thirteenth century (Torelli, *L'Archivio capitolare della Cattedrale di Mantova*, p. 180); an Andrea *fornexarius* and a Pelatus *fornexarius* appear in a document of 1303 (Torelli, *Ibid.*, p. 380), and a Bilaqua *fornexarius*, in a document of 1321 (Torelli, *Ibid.*, p. 479).

[1] *Ibid.*, pp. 27 ff., 52-54.

parents had a horror of bestowing on a Christian
lad at baptism the name of the Pagan Poet commonly regarded as a magician. Therefore, the name
given to the ditch is doubtless that of the Poet. All
this is proof that the occupants of the Fornicata
estate near the territory of Pietole, as well as their
neighbors, in the early years of the eleventh century cherished a lively remembrance of their great
compatriot. That ditch would have recalled to
them the anecdote told by Donatus — whether true
or fictitious matters little — about the birth of
Virgil.[1]

Another Virgilian tradition that we find at Pietole is that of the poplar-tree (*pioppo* or *pioppa*) of
Virgil; this tradition extended down to the eighteenth century, when the poplar had already disappeared. There was much uncertainty about its
precise situation.[2] This tradition also had its roots
in the *Life* by Donatus, and perhaps in its last
source, the *Life* by Suetonius.[3]

In the fifteenth century a little hill situated at
the boundary between the parish of Cerese and
that of Pietole was called Mount Virgilius; on this
hill was a very old house which was shown to visi-
tors as the house of the Poet. That the name *Mons
Virgilius* was popularly used is attested by its men-

[1] See above, p. 19.
[2] Cf. Carreri, pp. 18–19, 29, 66.
[3] See above, pp. 20 f.

tion in a document of the thirteenth century in the
Gonzaga Archives, and this notice is corroborated
by a document of 1420 in the "Libro Maestro" of
the Hospital of Mantua,[1] also by the author of the
life of Vittorino da Feltre,[2] by G. Gibellino in the
Life of Pius the Second,[3] by Giovanni Bremio,[4] and
by others.

[1] The document of the Gonzaga Archives cited by Carreri
(*De luco*, p. 9) reads: "Addimus huic vinee Iohannes [*sic*] de
Saca de Monte Virgilii que reddit fictum XVIII imp. et de-
cimam." That in the Hospital (Carreri, *Pietole*, etc., p. 10;
De luco, p. 10): reads "Mons Virgilii territorii Cerexii: una
pecia terre vineate unius bubulce posita in dictis territorio et
contrata penes . . . et viam versus lacum." *Montsèi*, "little
mountains," is the name given today by the people to heights
round about the Napoleonic fort at Pietole, near the banks of
the Mincio.

[2] Fr. Prendilacqua, *De vita Victorini Feltrensis* (Patavii,
1774), p. 86: "Constat tamen (Victorinum) parvum in subur-
banis hortum pauculis vitibus refertum pecuniaque ab eo con-
ductum possedisse, antiqui Poetae nostri domum atque sedem,
in qua natum illum cives nostri gloriantur. Hunc civitati proximum cum discipulis venerationis gratia frequentavit. Virgilii
montem incolae appellant, aliquanto ceteris eminentiorem
atque in collis altitudinem porrectum." Prendilacqua was one
of the pupils of Vittorino.

[3] Quoted by Carreri, p. 14.

[4] Jo. Bremii *Quisquiliae* (in *P. Verg. Mar. Opera* [Milan,
1520]), fol. X: "Voluptas (honestam puto) loci videndi, illuc
me aliquando duxit. Cumque a pagi habitatore quodam, quem
ut id faceret, rogaveram, in agrum quem Poetae fuisse dicebant,
ibidemque natum, deductus essem, ibi etiam ruinae quaedam
domus videbantur, non sine magna admiratione singula con-
siderabam; videbarque interdum tantum infantem cernere et
conspectum colere. Horror insuper venerabilis admirantem in-
vaserat, qualis sanctum templum lucosque divinos subeuntem
capit. Locum appellant incolae Montem Vergilii, qui cum ad
Mintii ripam sit, a quo iactu lapidis valido lacerto iacti distet,

With this tradition of the Mount of Virgil is also linked the one about the beech of Virgil popularly called Roverone.[1]

These two traditions, I believe, have an important bearing on certain passages in the ancient commentators that have not received the attention they deserve. The first is the note of Servius on verse 47 of the *First Eclogue: "Quamvis lapis omnia nudus."* He comments: "Id est quamvis mons sit et lacus: nam a monte usque ad lacum et inde usque

sitque iter sursus versus faciendum et ascensu superandus fluminis alveus, cognovi propertea montem esse ab illis dictum, cum tamen nullus ibi mons habeatur. Illa utique forma visa est, quam de agro ipso, Ecloga nona, Poeta his versibus complexus est: Certe equidem audieram, etc."

An English traveller of the sixteenth century records the following in his diary (British Museum, Egerton MS. 2146, fol. 17, cited by Carreri, *Pietole*, etc., p. 14): "From Mantoa we went by water downe the river Meltio [*sic*] and afterwarde we entered into the Poo as far as Ferrara, and from thence we went to Padoa by land. Wittin ii or iii miles of Mantoa there is a village called Pietola where Virgile was born and upon the hill there is a little bricke house which thin habitants of the countrey call *Casetta di Virgilio*, holding opinioun that was his house and that there he kept his beastes as a shepperd."

[1] Cf. Carreri, pp. 17, 31. The legend of the *Roverone* is attested by an old map of the estate called La Virgiliana which was seen by Carreri and until not many years ago was preserved in that place. Today the map has disappeared. The old tree stood between La Virgiliana and Formaielle (part of the ancient Fornicata estate), near Fossegone, a ditch that collected the water of the lowland surrounding La Virgiliana. The name "Oak Meadow" or "Oak Plain" (*prato* or *pianone della rovere*) still survives. In a document of 1303 (Torelli, *op. cit.*, pp. 379 ff.) the "contrata Cerri" (bitter oak) is mentioned several times.

ad arborem quandam, fuerat Arrio donata tua pos-
sessio."

In this comment, repeated almost literally by
Philargyrius,[1] three things are to be noted: the
mons, he *lacus*, the *arbor*, which are the three
points that determine the triangle within which
Servius places the property of Virgil. Further, the
mountain can be none other than the *Mons Virgilii*
of popular tradition, and this for a very simple
reason — that it is situated not far from the lake.
The lake, moreover, is called by Servius and Philargyrius Virgil's swamp;[2] it is Dante's "lama," the
lowland that the broadening Mincio turns into a
marsh.[3] Now it is known that both in the time of
Virgil and in that of Servius, that is, before the
great hydraulic works of the architect Pitentino at
the beginning of the thirteenth century, the Mincio
did not form a lake except at the southeast of Man-

[1] On *Ecl.* I, 47 (Thilo and Hagen, III, 2, 23): "QUAMVIS
LAPIS, idest quamvis mons sit et lacus. Nam a monte usque ad
lacum et inde usque ad arborem quandam fuerat terra donata."

[2] See Servius's laconic comments on *Ecl.* I, 48: "PALUS, id est
aequor. OBDUCAT, id est tegat. IUNCO, id est faeno vel fluvio
Mincio." Philargyrius has virtually the same notes, even in
Hagen's imperfect edition; in some ancient codices studied by
Funaioli, the *palus Virgiliana* is identified directly with the
flumen Mincii. Commenting on the expression *ad aquam* of
Eclogue IX, 9, Servius notes: "*Mincio fluminis scilicet.*"

[3] *Inferno*, XX, 77:

> "Non piu Benaco, ma Mincio si chiama
> Fino a Governo, dove cede in Po.
> Non molto ha corso, che trova una lama,
> Nella qual si distende la impaluda."

tua, just where popular tradition has placed Andes.
The *arbor* mentioned in the comments of Servius
and Philargyrius was clearly understood by them
to have been a beech. On *Ecl.* IX, 9, where some
manuscript or manuscripts of his day must have
read *fagi* for *fagos*, Philargyrius notes on this "old
beech":

"FAGI, idest, sicut superius dictum est, a lacu
usque ad arborem fines possessionis Vergilii a triumviris divisoribus agri Mantuani esse indultos."[1]

3. *The Adversaries of the Tradition of Pietole*

In the Middle Ages, no one, so far as I know,
ever expressed any doubt that Pietole,[2] the ancient

---

[1] Thilo and Hagen, III, 2, 169.

[2] A wood-cut of the ancient village made in 1900 is reproduced in the Frontispiece from a photograph by the firm of
Premi, Mantua. On the land where the ancient village stood
there has been recently formed a group of houses that has taken
the name of *Pietolvecchio.*

A stone pillar marks the spot where stood the parish church.
The name Pietole (*Pletulae*) is not derived from *Pievettole,*
double diminutive of *Pieve* (*Plebs*) as was held by G. B. Intra,
Mantova ne'suoi monumenti di storia e d'arte (Mantova, 1883),
p. 171, and after him by A. Dal Zotto, *op. cit.*, p. 229. It comes
rather from *plictula* or *plectula,* which seems to denote either a
bend in the river near which the *pagus* was situated or a street
that ran along the stream. A careful examination of the mediaeval documents in which Pietole is mentioned induces one to
believe that the name was originally *Plectula* or *Pletula,* singu-
lar number, and that the plural form is due to a phonetic law
observable in place-names of the region, whereby proparoxy-
tones tend to change final *a* to *e.* Examples of this law in the
Mantuan district are Medole, Quingentole, Nosedole, etc.

village, now destroyed, rising on a little height near the banks of the Mincio, a little less than two kilometers north of the modern village, was the ancient Andes, where Virgil was born. The statement of Probus, supplemented by that of Servius and of Philargyrius, fully supported the tradition, as we have seen. Donizzone, however, eager to deprive Mantua of her glory, doubts if the tradition is true.[1]

The first who opposed the tradition was Scipio Maffei, in 1732. He, basing his theory on the appellation "Venetian" given to the Poet by Macrobius, sought Andes, and naturally found it, at Bande, a part of the town of Cavriana, about thirty-five kilometers from Mantua, on the morainic hills which enclose Lake Garda, near the present boundary between Mantua and Verona.

The Mantuan historian, Visi, a faithful but not always discriminating collector of the legends of his country, undertook to re-examine the question, with the intention of combating the thesis of Maffei. He held that Virgil was born at Mantua, as the

When and in consequence of what events the name of Andes disappeared along with so many other Celtico-roman names is difficult to prove. Possibly Pietole is nothing else than a barbarian village that sprang up on the ruins of the ancient Andes, or in its immediate vicinity, during the period of the Germanic invasions. Possibly, also, it was situated in the "abandoned valley" mentioned in documents of the thirteenth century, as I shall show below.

[1] Donizzone, *Vita Mathildis* (in Muratori, *Rerum Italicarum Scriptores*, V, 360).

epitaph on the Poet's tomb would show, but that he must have had property on the Mincio, toward Rivalta, where the rising ground recalls the sloping of the hills in the *Ninth Eclogue*, *"usque ad aquam."*[1]

In 1848 Keil made a new critical edition of Probus's *Life of Virgil* and his commentary.[2] The text of Keil served as a basis for Reifferscheid and for Hagen. It looked like the end of the Pietole tradition: the critical text of Probus placed Andes at thirty Roman miles from Mantua. Mommsen, in volume V of the *Corpus Inscriptionum Latinarum*, and Hülsen, in the encyclopaedia of Pauly-Wissowa, accepted as definitive the distance indicated by Probus.

Where, then, was Andes? Monsignor A. Besutti and Professor R. Seymour Conway have recently undertaken to find it.

Monsignor Besutti[3] has revived the thesis of Maffei combined with that of Visi. Andes is Bande; but the parents of Virgil were from the city of Mantua. Since they had possessions in Andes, they had gone there; and there the Poet was born, by chance. This does not preclude the fact that Virgil was thoroughly Mantuan, as Besutti notes, although Maffei vainly imagined that he had proved

---

[1] Visi, *Notizie storiche della città e dello stato di Mantova* (1781–82), I, 30–31.

[2] Keil, *M. Valerii Probi in Verg. Buc. et Georg. commentarius*, Halle, 1848.

[3] *La Patria di Virgilio*, Asola (Mantua), 1927.

the contrary. The arguments used to sustain this thesis are in substance the same as those used by Maffei, with an added comparison of the landscape pictured in the *First* and the *Ninth Eclogue* with that of Bande.

Professor Seymour Conway[1] places the farm where Virgil was born, at Calvisano beyond the Chiese, in the province of Brescia. According to him, the Pietole tradition originated in the rediscovery of an inscription (considered apocryphal by Mommsen) under the altar of the greater church of this village.[2] The tradition was maintained for subsequent centuries, thanks, in great part, to the authority of Dante. Conway asserts that if it were true, almost all the information that Virgil gives us in the *Eclogues* about his farm would be "absurdly false." To demonstrate his thesis, he uses two arguments. The first is derived from a curious coincidence. At Calvisano there was found an inscription, perhaps of the Augustan era, in which the name of a certain *Vergilia* appears. At Casalpoglio on the Chiese there was discovered another inscription

---

[1] *Where was Virgil's Farm?* (in *Atene e Roma*, N.S., VII, 3 (July-Sept. 1926), O. 170–186. See also his final statement of the case in *The Vergilian Age* (Cambridge, Mass.: Harvard University Press, 1928), pp. 14–40.

[2] *C. I. L.*, vol. V, 3827 b.: P. Vergilio Pont. Max. Sabin. Differing from Mommsen, Conway considers that this inscription proves — and this is a grave admission for him — that some member of the *gens Vergilia* was at one time honored at Pietole.

with the name *P. Magius*, name of the *gens* to
which the maternal grandfather of the Poet belonged.[1] Now Calvisano is thirty Roman miles
from Mantua, as Probus asserts. Conway's second
argument is taken from the customary comparison
of the country described in the *Eclogues*[2] with the
landscape of Calvisano and of Pietole.

Of all the arguments accumulated against the
popular tradition, which also has some foundation
in the biographers and the scholiasts, the only one
of any weight, I think, is that which is based on the
text of Probus as given by Keil and Hagen. But of
this we have already spoken. The other arguments
are too feeble to weaken a tradition of many centuries.

Further, the appeal to Macrobius has little point.
Servius, the contemporary of Macrobius, regarded
even Mantua as Venetian.[3]

Nor does Conway's first argument prove much.
It is enough to observe that the name *Vergilius* recurs also in other inscriptions coming from different localities of the tenth Augustan region, very far
from Calvisano; and that the name *Magius* is still
more frequent, as can be seen at a glance from the
index to volume V of the *Corpus Inscriptionum
Latinarum*.

[1] Cf. above, p. 9.
[2] I; III, 12; V, 8, 63; VII; IX.
[3] Cf. above, p. 15.

On the other hand, the argument drawn from the comparison of the landscape of the *Bucolics* with that of Pietole and with that of Bande and of Calvisano, requires a lengthier consideration.

First of all, Besutti and Conway say nothing of the fact that the Mantuan territory has undergone profound modificationfrom what it was in the time of Virgil and also that of Servius. The principal cause of this modification is the changed courses of the rivers. The Mincio, which now has only one bed and which empties into the Po at Governolo, not improbably was divided into two streams, as in the Middle Ages, before reaching Mantua. One branch would have emptied into the Larione, after uniting with the Osone and crossing the lowlands over which the Fossa Viva now runs. Its other branch skirted the city, forming, as it does today, an arc from northwest to southeast and spreading in a swampy valley that Livy[1] calls "*Stagnum effusum Mincio amni.*" We may suppose that from there it also surrounded the city on the southwest and the south with a third branch that pushed its way through the valley of the Paiolo. This, however, cannot be proved. It is absolutely unlikely, at any rate, that the valley of the Paiolo was occupied by the "*stagnum*" of which Livy speaks. If it is permissible to gather data for reconstruction from present height-measurements, the "*palus*" of Virgil

[1] XXIV, 10, 7.

and the "*stagnum*" of Livy could have lain only in the valleys of Pietole, and, in particular, round about La Virgiliana and certain spots along the Lago Inferiore. On beyond Mantua, the Mincio joined the Fissero in the neighborhood of Governolo and together with it emptied into the Tartaro and thence into a branch of the Po, not far from its outlet.

The Po, not yet closely confined by strong embankments to a single channel, was divided into several streams and flowed much farther towards the south than in its course today. Strabo, who tells of the swamps that from the Po to Etruria blocked the march of Hannibal,[1] places Mantua, nevertheless, among the Transpadane cities that were situated "far above the marshes."[2] The displacement of the Po at Mantua is due on the one hand to the sediment accumulated from its Apennine tributaries and on the other to the gentle depression of the Padane region in its central zone. Documents of the twelfth century clearly distinguish the old from the new course of the Po, which in the twelfth century emptied its waters into the Larione, in whose bed they were securely contained by means of embankments that succeeding generations constantly re-enforced.[3]

[1] V, 1, 11.

[2] V, 1, 6–7.

[3] On the ancient hydrography of the Mantuan terrain, see E. Paglia, *Saggio di studi naturali sul territorio mantovano*, Man-

Meanwhile the Mincio, owing to the breaches
of the Adige (the first of all in 589), was blocked
from a free course to the Fissero and the Tartaro;
it thus had to force a new path to the east of
Governolo, making its way, like the Po — we know
not precisely at what time, but certainly considerably before the twelfth century — into the Larione.
But so soon as the waters of the latter were swollen
with those of the Po, which had abandoned its
ancient bed, there started, in seasons of flood, a series of overflows that, proceeding along the Mincio
from Governolo, invaded the Mantuan plain and
little by little converted it into a swamp. In the
days of Catullus the Mincio had had a tranquil and
perennial course, rising on its highest level not more
than ten meters above the sea; it could be navigated
from the Adriatic to Lake Garda by that *"phase-
lus"* which had braved the storms of the Aegean
and the rude Pontic Sea. But now the river began
to raise the level of its bed by the overflows of the
muddy water of the Po-Larione, and to invade, in
time of flood, the valleys around Mantua. In this
way the city was ultimately surrounded on every

tova, 1897; Filiasi, *Memorie storiche dei Veneti primi e secondi*
Padova, 1811; Lombardini, *Intorno al sistema idraulico del Po,·
ai principali cambiamenti che ha subito*, etc., Milano, 1840
*Idem, Della condizione idraulica della pianura subappennina fra
l'Enza e il Panaro*, Milano, 1865; Averone, *Sull'antica idrografia
veneta*, Mantova, 1911. Other authors who have concerned
themselves with this subject are mentioned below in the citations of their works.

side by insalubrious swamps, which occasioned
the first great work of the architect Pitentino,
voted by the town towards the end of the twelfth
century and designed to control the force of the
waters that overflowed from the new course of the
Po. In two documents of the first half of the thirteenth century, mention is made of a "*vallis aban-
donata*," namely at Pietole.[1] This is sure evidence
that the steady increase of the water obliged the
inhabitants to abandon the cultivation of the lowlands near the Mincio and to repair to the higher
ground.

These highlands are formed, as is well known,
from fluvio-glacial terrain, that is to say, from the
débris of the great moraine that encloses Lake
Garda, carried down by the force of the water re-
leased by the melting of the glacier. Between these
hillocks the Mincio had dug out a channel of consid-
erable depth, so that their elevations, if observed
from the bank of the stream, appeared to rise above
the normal level of the water noticeably more than
they do today; they might well have been called,
and they were called, ridges, hills, or small mountains (*monticelli, monticuli*). Today the difference
between the height of these ridges and the level of
the stream has decreased by several meters, not
only because of the rising of the water but also because of two facts that it is well to bear in mind.

[1] Torelli, *L'Archivio capitolare*, pp. 95, 180.

The first is that in recent times the configuration of the land has been altered by the construction of fortifications and of the embankment that runs from the Fort of Pietole to La Virgiliana. The other fact is a more ancient affair and is due to natural forces.

Once upon a time the wayfarer who passed along the banks of the Mincio and looked up at the heights of Pietole saw them clothed with the woods and copses that at the end of the Middle Ages were beginning to be cut down. The existence of ample tracts of woodland in the plain of the Po and, in particular, between the left bank of the Po and the right bank of the Mincio, near Mantua, is plainly attested by mediaeval documents. Thus a document of 870 and another of 880 mention woods situated "*inter Padum et Zaram.*"[1] Others of 961 and 1110 mention the "*silva mantuana.*"[2] Another of 962 speaks of "*Silvae et buscalia . . . iuxta fluvio Padi.*"[3] In one of 1012 there is notice of a "*terra silvata . . . super fluvio Padi in fundo Septingenti.*"[4] In the environs of Pietole there is mention of the "*silva Armanore.*"[5] The estate of Governolo, at that time situated on the right bank of the Mincio, included "*de gerbidis et silvis iuges* DC" in contrast to 400 *iuges* of tilled land; similarly the estate of

---

[1] Torelli, *Regesto Mantovano* (Rome, 1914), I, 8, 12.
[2] *Ibid.*, pp. 18, 432.
[3] *Ibid.*, p. 20. [4] *Ibid.*, p. 34.
[5] Document of 1014, *ibid.*, p. 35.

Castelnuovo, near Curtatone, contained "*de ger-bidis et silvis iuges* MCD" over against 600 *iuges* of tilled land.[1] Another document mentions the "*sil-vas de Bagnolo iuxta Mencium.*"[2] In the immediate vicinity of Pietole, an estate described as "*domus cultilis que vocatur Fornicata*" is credited with "*de buscaleis iuges* MMM" but with only 32 *iuges* of tilled land.[3] Finally, from a document of 1113 we may infer what sorts of vegetation, among others, flourished in these woods, since in this deed the Countess Matilde concedes to the monastery of St. Benedict that "*in unoquoque anno de bosco Bag-nolo. XII. inter robores et ceros tolant.*"[4] And in Pietole we find record of a "*contrata Cerri,*"[5] which might be that around the Roverone of which we have already spoken.[6] Little by little, as the fields once uninhabited began to be peopled, it was necessary to reduce these woodland tracts bit by bit — in our day they have disappeared altogether — to secure space for arable soil. Thus vanished the woods that with their umbrageous crests increased the height of the little hills for one who looked at them from the valley below. Then for more than eight centuries the rains fell on land that was worked and constantly shifted; for man's labor tends to level mounds of earth and to fill in the low

[1] Document of 1044, p. 47.   [2] Document of 1077–91, p. 84.
[3] Document of 1072, p. 65.   [4] *Ibid.*, p. 113.
[5] Torelli, *L'Archivio capitolare,* pp. 279–281.
[6] See above, p. 122.

places. This will suffice to show how the country
of Pietole has lost today the bucolic character that
it has in the pastoral poems of Virgil.[1]

A second observation is suggested to me by an
ancient comment cited by Servius. In verses 7 to
10 of the *Ninth Eclogue*, did Virgil mean to describe
only his farm or all the territory about Mantua?
If it is true, as some scholars think[2] that when Virgil
went to Rome he interceded not only for himself
but for all his unfortunate compatriots who likewise had been robbed of their lands, it would not
be at all surprising if in the verses cited, the Poet
should mention all the Mantuan territory over
which the decree of confiscation had extended. Certainly there is an idea of vastness in *omnia vestrum
servasse Menalcan* that renders the ancient comment highly probable.

Finally, a word on the scenery in the *Bucolics*.
There is almost always an Alexandrine or Theocritean background in Virgil's pastoral pictures,
even when they contain impressively realistic details. If this is less clear in *Tityrus*, where, nevertheless, slight echoes of Theocritus occur,[3] it is

----

[1] One detail is of much importance — or should be — for
certain opponents of the Pietole tradition. The Mincio, Virgil's
river *par excellence*, is found neither at Calvisano nor at Bande.
Conway evidently did not observe this. Besutti does; so besides the farm at Bande, he presents Virgil with another near
Mantua, "on the edge of the lake that surrounds the city"
(p. 20). So here we are again at Pietole, or thereabouts!

[2] See above, p. 88, n. 3 and p. 92, n. 2.

[3] Cf. above, p. 89.

obvious in *Moeris*, the scheme of which is taken from Theocritus.[1] Tityrus himself, though experiences of Virgil are attributed to him, is a purely bucolic character, like Moeris and Menalcas.

With this device, has Virgil struck a false note? No, he has idealized the reality, rounding off its angles. For true art is not born until the violence of impressions has subsided and the imagination recovers its power serenely to create.

If Conway and Besutti had taken account of these qualities of the mind they perhaps would not have urged the flimsy evidence drawn from the landscape of the *Bucolics*. We need quite different proofs to demolish a tradition so deeply rooted as that which has gathered about Pietole, where alone in all the districts of Mantua or the neighboring communities Virgilian memories of a popular character are preserved. Pietole would not be less amazed, I believe, at seeing the glory of Virgil snatched from her than would Bande and Calvisano at having it bestowed upon themselves.[2]

---

[1] Cf. above, pp. 95 f.

[2] Among the adversaries of the Pietole traditions we are compelled to place Attilio Dal Zotto. His learned arguments on the matter are too complicated to be discussed at this point; they will be answered elsewhere.

APPENDIX II

THE CONFISCATION OF LANDS

FROM the swarm of statements collected by the early biographers and commentators of Virgil it is immediately evident that they have not represented in a uniform manner the sequence of facts mentioned in the *First* and the *Ninth Eclogue*. It is worth while to pause and consider their evidence to see wherein they agree and wherein they differ.

Beginning with Probus, we remember that he placed the *Ninth Eclogue* before the *First*.[1] In his *Life* he asserts that the confiscation took place after the battle of Modena, and that Virgil was reinstated "*beneficio Alfeni Vari, Asinii Pollionis et Cornelii Galli.*"[2] However, in the preface to the *Bucolics* he places the confiscation after Actium (!) and attributes the credit of the reinstallation solely to Cornelius Gallus, the fellow-pupil of Virgil.[3] Hinting at the danger run by Virgil, he asserts that the Poet had so enraged the veterans, "*ut a Milieno Torone primipilari paene sit interfectus, nisi fugisset.*"[4]

[1] *Praef. ad Bucol.* (Thilo and Hagen, III, 2, 328): "Prius fuit queri damnum, deinde testari beneficium."
[2] Brummer, p. 73.
[3] Thilo and Hagen, III, 2, 327 f.
[4] *Ibid.*, p. 328.

Donatus, after declaring that Virgil wrote the *Bucolics* to honor Asinius Pollio, Alfenus Varus, and Cornelius Gallus, who had saved him from the confiscation, which occurred after Philippi,[1] goes back on his statement and places the confiscation at the end of the civil war which broke out after the murder of Caesar, that is, after the battle of Modena. Caesar, according to him, had caused the territory of Cremona to be invaded by the veterans because the people of Cremona had been partisans of Antony.[2] Then he relates how Virgil was saved from the confiscation and from the threats of Arrius.[3]

Servius agrees in substance with the second version of Donatus. He also makes Pollio and Maecenas champion the cause of Virgil.[4] The episode of the centurion Arrius is also narrated by him in the same manner.[5]

Servius Danielis, however, is acquainted with circumstances unknown to Donatus and to the real Servius; his information has all the appearance of coming from reliable sources. He makes the confiscation of the lands of Virgil fall within the time in which Alfenus Varus, at the end of the Perusine

[1] Brummer, p. 5.
[2] Brummer, p. 15.
[3] See above, pp. 92 f.
[4] *Vita* (Brummer, p. 69); *Prooem. in Bucol.* (Thilo and Hagen, III, 1, 2-3).
[5] *Prooem. in Bucol.* (*op. cit.*, p. 3); *Ecl.* III, 94; *Ecl.* IX, 1.

War, succeeded Pollio in the government of Cisalpine Gaul.[1]

Servius Danielis also reports the opinion of those
who make Pollio responsible for Virgil's exemption
from the loss of his lands, but offers it as simply an
opinion. Besides, he assigns to Gallus the office of
collector of tributes from the municipalities of the
Transpadane countries which had been immune
from confiscation;[2] and gives us the gist of a speech
of Cornelius (Gallus?) in which Alfenus Gallus was
accused of not having left to the Mantuans even
the usual three miles of territory around the
city.[3] The quarrel to which the *Ninth Eclogue* refers
must have occurred about a question of boundary
between Virgil and a certain Clodius, who drew his
sword, forcing the Poet to take refuge in the shop
of a charcoal dealer.[4] Finally, the commentator
mentions the name of Octavius Musa as *limitator*,
entrusted by Octavian with the measuring of the
confiscated lands. He is said to have been very
severe with the Mantuans because they had en-
closed one of his flocks of sheep in the public field.[5]

The *Scholia Bernensia* agree with Servius Danielis. They have an unimportant variant about
the episode of Octavius Musa.[6]

---

[1] *Ecl.* IX, 27–28; VI, 6. Cf. *Scholia Bernensia, Ecl.* VI, 7.
[2] *Ecl.* VI, 64.   [3] *Ecl.* IX, 10.
[4] *Ecl.* IX, 1.   [5] *Ecl.* IX, 7.
[6] *Scholia Bernensia, Ecl.* VIII, 6.

Printed in the USA
CPSIA information can be obtained
at www.ICGtesting.com
LVHW020828261124
797559LV00003B/593